John Saul Howson, Alfred Rimmer

The River Dee

Its aspect and history

John Saul Howson, Alfred Rimmer

The River Dee
Its aspect and history

ISBN/EAN: 9783337233235

Printed in Europe, USA, Canada, Australia, Japan

Cover: Foto ©ninafisch / pixelio.de

More available books at **www.hansebooks.com**

THE RIVER DEE

ITS ASPECT AND HISTORY

By J. S. HOWSON, D.D.

DEAN OF CHESTER

AND

ALFRED RIMMER

WITH NINETY-THREE ILLUSTRATIONS ON WOOD

FROM DRAWINGS BY ALFRED RIMMER

LONDON

J. S. VIRTUE & CO., LIMITED, 26, IVY LANE

PATERNOSTER ROW

1889.

LONDON:
PRINTED BY J. S. VIRTUE AND CO., LIMITED.
CITY ROAD.

PREFACE.

N revising these pages for separate publication I have been made very conscious, both of the excellence and charm of their subject on the one hand, and, on the other hand, of the very inadequate and unworthy manner in which the subject is here treated. It would be a most pleasant task to me, if sufficient health and opportunity were granted to me, to endeavour to do more justice to the scenery and history of this river; but many difficulties impeded even the writing of these short chapters; and I have been compelled in some degree to modify their original plan and arrangement, especially as regards the Estuary. Under these circumstances my friend Mr. Rimmer had the goodness to write the Tenth and Eleventh Chapters, having reference to the architectural topics, with which he is professionally conversant.

J. S. II.

COLWYN BAY, *July 17th*, 1875.

PREFACE.

ITH reference to the brief Preface which was written by the late Dean Howson, it may be said that he contemplated an enlarged edition, with many subjects added that he could not include in his first limits; and now, of course, such a hope is past. We had expected to spend a summer holiday among the hills of the Dee, and follow some of its feeders up to their mountain fastnesses. From Llandullo to Corwen is some four or five miles, and the scenery is a happy mixture of the beautiful and the grand. Corwen is a quiet market-town, with the Berwyn hills rising almost abruptly behind; and there it was our wish to have explored, and gone through mountain roads as far as Montgomery, which, in a direct line, is not more than three miles distant; and this county never approaches nearer the Dee.

The quaint old chapel of Rûg, also near Corwen, is worth not only a visit, but almost a pilgrimage. Its ancient carvings and frescoes are fast perishing, but they speak of its former elaboration and richness; and it stands in what may be called valley scenery of unsurpassed beauty.

We had hoped also to have said much more about Owen Glendower, a character that is almost as romantic as any in the range of history. The almost lurid light in which Shakespeare makes him appear in *Henry IV.* is confirmed by Sharon Turner in his " History of the Middle Ages." His desire to be friendly with Hotspur at any price, and his long forbearance with the haughty rejoinders of the future head of the Percys, are all in keeping with the character, more recently drawn, of this Welsh chieftain. It is probable he quite believed in the prodigies that he affirmed had occurred at his birth; and Mortimer and Percy said no more than truth when they affirmed that the man was not alive that might so have tempted him. The table which appears in the book at page 33, and is called "Glendower's Dining-table," may certainly be correctly so named, as its great weight and size would indicate that it must have belonged to the neighbourhood. It could not have been brought from London, and there was no Birmingham; and the farmhouse where it daily dines the labourers, and is not full even at harvest-time, is within the limits of Glendower's castle-rights. It is English in form, and quite illustrates the final scenes of his life. Glendower, when he could not restrain his anger against Hotspur, said—

> " I can speak English, lord, as well as you:
> For I was brought up in the English court,
> Where, being but young, I framed upon the harp
> Many an English ditty, lovely well,
> And gave the tongue a helpful ornament;
> A virtue that was never seen in you."

We had hoped, indeed, to throw some more light upon Glendower and his fitful life, and, still even more, to do justice to the beautiful country that is identified with his history.

The Vale of Llangollen has changed somewhat since the first edition of this book appeared, and mines and quarries are bringing in a population that consorts little with its ancient claims to beauty. Still, these are only local, and a mile or two brings us into the pleasant old valley in any direction.

Chester was fairly well represented in the first edition; and, as Dean Howson says, two chapters out of twelve were as much as could fairly be claimed for it, even though so much was left unsaid.

The visit of the Archæological Society, which is occurring while these pages are written, was a cherished wish of Dean Howson, and he arranged it with the President in the year before his death. Many are the treasures they will be shown; and, indeed, there are men of middle age living in Chester that never saw the interior of the houses in Bridge Street Row, some of which contain rooms of great splendour, though they are turned into the humblest uses, even such as receptacles for old furniture and lumber-rooms.

The death of Dean Howson, though not sudden, caused a deep gloom in the city; and the sudden death of his wife only a fortnight after appalled the whole community. They were buried in the same grave in the beautiful cloisters of the Cathedral, the Secretary of State at once giving the required permission, though this is an exceptional favour to grant.

The late Dean graduated at Trinity College, Cambridge, and took a double first-class degree in 1836. In the following year he gained the Members' Prize, and also the Norrissian Prize Essay. He also became Hulsean Lecturer; and shortly after leaving college he was joint author with Dr. Conybeare of the "Life of St. Paul," a work that has long been regarded as a standard classic, and is quite as well known in America as it is in England. Among many other works he wrote a tiny volume of three sermons, called "Good and Bad Habits," free from all dogma, and abounding in sympathy. It was always considered a fortunate opening for the Liverpool College that the services of such brilliant scholars as Conybeare and Howson should be secured, as well as of Dr. Booth, who was the Professor of Mathematics, and at a comparatively early age was made a Fellow of the Royal Society. The Dean, from being first Master, became Principal of the College in 1849; and he held this office for sixteen years. His success as Principal was eminent. There are no better judges of character than boys. They are as a rule much freer from prejudice and worldly considerations, they have an innate sense of justice, and keenly appraise anything in the shape of favouritism;

yet we were all so thoroughly assured of his fairness and sympathy with every one, that it is not too much to say that in Liverpool College there was not a single scholar who did not regard him as a friend; and, indeed, any accident or misfortune—had any such ever befallen him—would have been as much a matter of solicitude to every scholar as if the mishap had fallen at his own home.

It was after a lengthened residence abroad that it was my privilege to renew his friendship, and among a number of other works we wrote together was this "River Dee." Our journeys along it were very pleasant, with many anecdotes and reminiscences of old times. I had the melancholy satisfaction of designing a sun-dial to his memory, and I cannot conclude this short retrospect better than by quoting an ancient inscription that surrounds the dial, indicating the days that have passed: "*Cito sed jucunde præteriere dies.*"

ALFRED RIMMER.

CHESTER, *October*, 1886.

CONTENTS.

———◆———

I.

INTRODUCTION.

VIII.

THE BRIDGES AND FERRIES OVER THE DEE.

IX.

THE ESTUARY.

X.

HALLS AND CASTLES ON THE DEE.

XI.

HALLS AND CASTLES ON THE DEE.

XII.

CONCLUSION.

LIST OF ILLUSTRATIONS.

LIST OF ILLUSTRATIONS.

I.

INTRODUCTION.

SPECIAL INTEREST OF RIVERS—THEIR CONNECTION WITH HUMAN LIFE—GREAT HISTORICAL RIVERS—STREAMS OF LESSER NOTE—DESCRIPTION OF THE MOSELLE BY AUSONIUS—CLAIM OF THE DEE ON OUR ATTENTION—ITS ATTRACTION FOR THE POETS—SPENSER—DRAYTON—MILTON.

RIVERS have an interest of their own, so special, yet so varied, so easily made a subject of separate and distinct thought, and yet touching other subjects of interest at so many points, that almost every river in the world deserves a careful description.

One obvious and attractive charm of a river is the extreme diversity of scenery through which it passes. How great, for instance, is the contrast between the rugged mountains or the bare moorlands, in the midst of which it takes its early birth, and the royal expanse of the estuary where in stately dignity it passes to the sea! And, intermediate between these extremes, how unceasing are the changes in the river's continuous existence, as it becomes, first a "tinkling rill," timidly running over its mossy bed, then a stream conscious, as it were, of its own importance, now dashing down over rocks in an eager waterfall, now "loitering in glassy pool," now winding in broad sunny reaches through rich meadows, now rippling over sloping beds of pebbles to cool places of silent shade deep under overhanging trees.

B

And at every point this continuous and diversified flow of water is in contact with some of the various phases of human life. The writer of these lines is thinking for the moment only of English rivers: and the scenes and objects which come successively before the imagination are such as these : a shepherd with his sheep dimly seen in the mountain-mist—a lonely fisherman exercising his patient craft—country people crossing the fords on their way to market— a small hamlet with its modest mill—larger villages where the idlers gather, on summer evenings, at the bridge—here the memorial of some famous battle-field—here the ivy-covered ruin of an ancient abbey—here the modern residence of a wealthy squire, with broad green acres and noble trees stretching down to the water-side—and farther on, as we approach some populous city, slow-moving barges with heavy traffic. At each moment of its progress such a river is an eloquent and instructive exponent of some features of our human existence. The more closely and the more thoughtfully the whole subject is considered, the more clearly it is seen to be full of Poetry.

Some rivers of other countries have a world-wide fame, which causes them to be universally recognised as worthy subjects of careful thought. Such is the Nile, with its immemorial history, its pyramids, its temples; its recollections, not simply of Moses and the Pentateuch, but of Alexander the Great, of Pompey the Great, of St. Louis, of Napoleon; and with its intense interest, at this very time, in connection with the heroism of geographical discovery. Such, on another continent, is the Ganges, alike because of the architecture of its cities, its old religious traditions, and because of its present close association with the fortunes of our own empire. Such also is the Mississippi, the great "Father of Waters," on a third continent, a river rich in the romance of the future, as those other rivers are rich in the romance of the past. Under the same class, to come nearer to our own home, we must, of course, include the Tiber—which in fact concentrates on its banks half the history of the world—and the Rhine, with its "frequent feudal towers," still

lifting through green leaves or on bare hillside " their walls of grey "
—each of them emphatically a river of the poets.

The purpose, however, of these chapters is to claim for waters
of lesser fame their just regard, and to show how much there is to
be loved and learnt in connection with one of our own domestic
streams

As an illustration of this feeling and of its expression, reference
may be made, in passing, to one river—not by any means one of the
most distinguished in Europe—not even having an independent and
complete course of its own, but merely a tributary—which has found
a poet, who from his enthusiasm and thorough appreciation of his
subject, may well be an example to any one who aspires to describe
a river. The stream in question is the Moselle, and the poet is
Ausonius. This author is by no means to be reckoned at a high
level among classic poets. In his " Idyll on the Moselle" he is often
turgid, exaggerated, and obscure. And yet it is a delightful poem to
read, especially on the banks of the river itself. The writer of these
pages remembers very well having had this pleasure in the public
library at Trèves, before going down the stream to Coblentz.
Ausonius tells us how his dear Moselle unites everything in itself—
fountain, river, lake, and sea. He describes the pellucid clearness of
the water, and speaks, not only of the moss and pebbles shining
through, with bright fish of all kinds darting among them, but of the
boatmen counting the very vine-leaves in the reflections of the
banks, as the boat floats idly down the stream. One fish must be
specially mentioned, because it seems to connect for us the Moselle
and the Dee; and perhaps this, and two other slight quotations, will
be pardoned, if given in Latin :—

> Nec te puniceo rutilantem viscere, Salmo,
> Transierim.

Great prominence is given in this poem to that exquisite greenness
of the banks of the Moselle, which must have struck every traveller
that has visited it in the early summer. Again and again Ausonius

speaks of these vineyards which rise now, as they rose then, in natural theatres up the sunny hillsides ; and he gives an animated picture of the jokes which passed at vintage-time between those who were engaged in gathering the grapes and the saucy foot-passengers on the road below. The whole scene too is full of that human interest which has been named above as eminently characteristic of the course of a river. We have presented to us in lively succession the boat-race, the fishing-rod, the houses of various architecture, in places of various choice, in sheltered nook, or on the edge of the water, or on high projecting headland. With such descriptions he follows the river from point to point, naming all the tributaries as they willingly fall in :

> Quamquam differre meatus
> Possent : sed celerant in te consumere nomen :

till at length the Rhine—"fraternis cumulandus aquis "—receives the Moselle, now become a tributary in turn, at that great " Confluence," which still retains its Latin designation. All this is done by this poet of the late Imperial times, with a rich appreciation of the significance of a river's progress : and at length, with a patriotic instinct, he closes his task by dedicating the Moselle to his native Garonne.

Among English rivers the Dee is well worthy of just such affectionate and discriminating treatment, especially on the part of those who dwell upon its banks. Next indeed after the Thames and the Severn, no river in this country can be named that is more worthy. The Dee has this double claim on our attention, that it is both a Welsh stream and an English stream. It possesses to the full the interest which belongs to every border-region. The whole range too of English history is lightly touched by circumstances connected with the Dee. In following its course we are in contact with the Druids, with the Romans, with the Saxons, with the Danes. The Norman Conquest has left its strong mark on the fortress which was long occupied by the Twentieth Legion : Chester was famous at many subsequent periods, especially in the war between King Charles and the Parliament; and from the estuary beyond the city fleets sailed for the West, when the great town on the Mersey was almost unknown. And, to turn to other points of interest, of the "Seven Wonders of Wales" four belong to the Dee. As regards beauty and dignity of outward aspect, the contrasts of mountain and meadow, of running water and calm sea, are well marked in the course of this short river. Its distinctive physical features and its natural history will, of course, come under review as we proceed. At present we may limit ourselves to the connection of our subject with Poetry.

The Dee has been, to a singular extent, a favourite with the English Poets: and this in reference to one peculiar characteristic which is supposed to belong to it. Whether it be from some reminiscence of the Druids, or from whatever cause, the "holiness" of this "wizard stream" meets us at every turn: so that a sacred mystery seems to brood over its waters, which belongs to no other stream in England.

Spenser makes mention of the Dee in two passages of the "Faërie Queene," which will be quoted hereafter. In one case he takes note of the source of the river in connection with early legend, and in language which almost makes us suspect that he was acquainted with the spot. In the other case it is as the River of Chester that it attracts his attention. Whether any circumstances caused Spenser to be conscious of some peculiar charm in this river, it may now be impossible to ascertain. This however we do know, that he must have passed this way, when he went to Ireland.

Reference must of course be made to Drayton. His "Polyolbion" will inevitably be our frequent companion in a description of the Dee, as would be the case with an attempt to handle any part of the archæology and topography of England, especially where rivers demand careful attention. Drayton's poetry, considered merely as poetry, may not rise to a very high level; but, for his time, he has a wonderful appreciation of the power of rivers, if closely studied, to lead us on to a correct view of the physical geography of a country: and this remark is as true of the Dee, as of any other English stream which comes under his cognizance. For the present we may limit ourselves to such passages as deal with the general bearings of the subject, such as the fact that it is one of the boundary streams of Wales, or its relation to other Welsh rivers that rise in the same mountain-region, or that characteristic "holiness" which has been mentioned above.

In the Ninth Song, where Merioneth recounts her rivers, she makes this boast :—

> " The pearly Conway's head, as that of holy Dee,
> Renownèd rivers both, their rising have in me."

In the Eighth Song we find the Severn addressing Wales thus :—

> . . . . . " Myself and my dear brother Dee
> By Nature were the bounds first limited to thee."

The Tenth Song contains an enumeration of the tributaries of the Dee, which will be more to our purpose afterwards; but we may very fitly introduce here a passage that occurs after the mention of the latest of these affluents, which is close upon the City of Chester :—

> . . . . " Twice under earth her crystal head doth run :
> When instantly again Dee's holiness begun,
> By his contracted front and sterner waves, to shew
> That he had things to speak might profit us to know ;
> A brook that was suppos'd much business to have seen,
> Which had an ancient bound 'twixt Wales and England been,
> And noted was by both to be an ominous flood,
> That, changing of his fords, the future ill or good
> Of either country told, of either's war or peace,
> The sickness or the health, the dearth or the increase ;
> And that of all the floods of Britain, he might boast
> His stream in former times to have been honour'd most."

This curious fancy, that by some shifting of his stream this sacred river gave prophetic intimations, to the English or the Welsh, of coming weal or woe, finds a place also in the Fourth Song. Here, among other geographical personages, in a contest as to whether Lundy Island belongs to England or Wales, "Holy Dee" is introduced :—

> . . . . " whose pray'rs were highly priz'd,
> As one in heavenly things devoutly exercis'd ;
> Who, changing of his fords, by divination had
> Foretold the neighbouring folk of fortune good or bad,"

and who, true to his character, "his benediction sends" on the occasion of this solemn dispute. And once more, turning to the Eleventh Song, we must adduce a further allusion to this mystic sanctity of our famous Cheshire stream. Another noted river in this county, the Weaver, of course obtains a prominent place, in consequence of its close connection with the production of salt at "those two renowned Wyches, the Nant-Wyche and the North." Salt is used in sacrifices. Salt is a token of friendship. Thus the Weaver, in regard of these salt-works,—

> " Besides their general use, not had by him in vain,
> But in himself thereby doth holiness retain
> Above his fellow floods."

Hence this river became possessed, as it were, of a rival sanctity,—

> " And bare his name so far, that oft 'twixt him and Dee
> Much strife there hath arose in their prophetic skill."

And especially the relation of salt to health is introduced as another element in this claim to holiness. The "healthful virtues" of the Weaver were such that even the Sea-Gods had recourse to him for " physic in their need," and that " by his salts" he durst "assure recovery," when Thetis saw her Nereids sick and even Glaucus could not cure them.

Our business, however, is with the Dee ; and we must now turn our thoughts to a poet greater than Drayton, or even than Spenser.

It seems clear that Milton had a peculiar love for rivers, and that, among rivers, the Dee had a great attraction for him. Some personal illustrations, too, of each of these points can be given, if not from fact, at least from reasonable conjecture.

Those familiar lines, opening with the words " Rivers, arise," are felt to be very curious when we consider, not only the early age at which they were written, but the abrupt manner in which they start forth in the College exercise of which they form a part : and an ingenious Cambridge critic once hazarded the conjecture that Milton had some friend named " Rivers" at the University. This guess is proved to be highly probable : for, immediately after the time when this exercise was written, two brothers bearing this name were entered at Christ's College. It is not stated that either of these brothers was the eldest son, whereas the fact of primogeniture was then usually specified in the Admission Books of that College. Moreover in those days families seem to have been more exclusively attached to particular colleges than is the case now. It appears highly probable that the Rivers family, clearly one of some position and repute, patronised Christ's, and that the eldest son was there with Milton.

As to the feeling, then, of peculiar interest, with which he regarded the Dee, we have here a very definite explanation, derived from personal friendship : and other facts enable us to follow the same line of thought in connection with this subject. Two of Milton's most intimate friends were Edward King, who was with him at Christ's College, Cambridge, and Charles Diodati, of Trinity College, Oxford, who had been his earlier companion at St. Paul's School. The loss of the former by the sinking of a vessel off the coast beyond Chester became the occasion of the poem of "Lycidas;" and in this poem the intense feeling is evident, with which Milton's mind was drawn to the mountain-region, where " the old Bards, the ancient Druids, lie," and where—

> " Deva spreads her wizard stream."

Youthful friendship formed also another link between Milton and this river. We need not enquire whether it is a true tradition that Charles Diodati had practised as a physician in Cheshire, when the poet, travelling in Italy, heard the terrible news of his death. This is hardly likely to have been the case: else the Dee would surely have found a place among the rivers which are named in the "Epitaphium Damonis." It is certain, however, that Diodati was here soon after leaving Oxford, and when he was beginning the study of medicine; and of this fact we have a record in the Latin verses, where Milton acknowledges a letter written to him by his friend :—

> "Occidua Devæ Cestrensis ab ora,
> Vergivium prono quà petit amne salum."

Nor is it foreign to our present train of thought to remark that in these lines, where he would have his friend to know that he is in London, and does not wish to return to Cambridge, he says, with his usual love of rivers, that he is in "the city which is washed by the reflux of the tide of the Thames," and that he has no desire to "revisit the reedy Cam."

It is not a little curious that Milton's third marriage should, after the lapse of more than thirty years, have brought him into close connection with Cheshire and the Dee, and that relics of the poet are even now remaining at that very Nant-Wyche which was named above.

II.

THE REGION OF THE SOURCE OF THE DEE—ITS RELATION TO GEOLOGY AND TO HISTORY —MOUNTAINS OF MEROINETHSHIRE—BALA LAKE—EARLIEST TRIBUTARIES OF THE DEE—CHILDHOOD OF KING ARTHUR—POSSIBLE WATER SUPPLY FROM BALA LAKE— "IDYLLS OF THE KING"—CHARLES OF BALA—CHARACTERISTICS OF WELSH ALPINE SCENERY.

IN this second chapter we may enter systematically on our survey of the course of the Dee; and our thoughts must be given, in the first place, to that great mountain region within which the river takes its rise, and which embraces Bala Lake (sometimes also called Lyn-Tegid, and sometimes Pimblemere), a sheet of water that—besides being the only lake of considerable size in Wales—impresses a marked character on the early, and indeed the later, progress of the Dee. In making this beginning, we shall be true to the geological facts of the primitive home of our river, and true also to the legends and earliest recorded history of the Welsh.

Geology must, in every case, determine, to a great extent, the outward aspect of a district. It is no part, however, of the present task to indicate more than very slightly this necessary connection. Of the region round the source of the Dee, it is enough to say, on this occasion, that it forms a conspicuous part of that "Cambrian" or "Silurian" system which is marked in the Annals of Science by the honoured labours and warm controversies of Sedgwick and Murchison. In subsequent chapters we shall have to trace the course of the stream through slates and shales of somewhat later formation, past Corwen, where the carboniferous limestone appears for a moment, and then across the belt of country where this limestone, in larger quantity, and in contact with the coal, produces industrial results very distinctly marked in the features of the landscape and the aspect of the population ; thence over that broad surface of New Red Sandstone, with its products of salt below and cheese above, which gives to Cheshire a most distinctive character of its own ; till the river, after passing Chester and turning westwards, opens out to the sea along the border of the coal again. In this chapter, however, we are limited to the consideration of earlier, in fact almost the earliest, slates and shales. The limestone which appears at Bala, and gives opportunity for useful occupation there—as does the carboniferous limestone at Corwen—belongs altogether to a different formation.

And if we turn now from Physical Science to Human Poetry and Biography, the region of the source of the Dee has the highest claims on our attention, in consequence of the hoar antiquity with which it is associated. The story of King Arthur is connected, as we shall see, in more ways than one with the rise of this sacred river, and with Bala Lake ; and passing onwards into history, if we could pursue its records in detail, we should find these mountains eloquent of heroic and romantic events in the reigns of Henry II., Edward I., and Henry IV., to say nothing of the indistinct echoes they give back to us of still earlier conflicts of the Britons with Saxons and with Romans.

Merioneth may truly be called the most Welsh of all the shires in Wales. It retains the old British name, which, in the case of some of the Welsh counties, has been lost. If no part of it rises to the very loftiest elevation attained in the western parts of our island, still Merionethshire includes the greatest number of mountain

summits. If Carnarvonshire can boast of the vast solid mass and
tremendous precipices of Snowdon, Merionethshire possesses Cader
Idris; and few mountains fill the view over a larger space and with
a more majestic outline. And—to revert for a moment to Geology
—where the western part of this county round Harlech Castle (to
use a phrase applied by Camden to Yorkshire) lies "sore on the sea,"
we have the very oldest rocks that are known in the world, with the
single exception of that Lauren-
tian system in Canada, which we
are proud to connect with the
names of two Transatlantic
geologists, Sir W. Logan and
Professor Dawson.

With the south-western slope
of the county towards Dolgelly
and Cader Idris we have, in these
pages, no direct concern. And
yet we can hardly help peering
over for a moment in this direction. Indeed, the pointed sum-
mit of Cader himself is visible,
and forms a distinguished part
of the fine mountain-view, from
the low ground near Bala Lake.
But, moreover, the great hero of
the upper waters of the Dee,
Owen Glendower, had much to do with Dolgelly, as we shall see in
the next chapter.   Our river, however, with the early tributaries that
flow into it, just above and just below the lake, belongs entirely to
the north-eastern slope.

Drayton, with a correct geographical and historical insight, introduces the mountains of Merionethshire with great pomp, and connects with them the waters of Bala Lake, referring at the same time

*Caer-Gai, an old Farmhouse at the head of
Bala Lake.*

to the struggles for Welsh independence that have been connected
with this region. His Ninth Song hath this preamble—

> " The Muse here Merioneth vaunts,
> And her proud mountains highly chaunts,
> The hills and brooks, to bravery bent,
> Stand for precedence from descent ;
> The rivers for them showing there
> The wonders of their Pimble-Mere."

And when he opens out his subject, it is in these lines—

> " Of all the Cambrian shires their heads that bear so high,
> And farth'st survey their soils with an ambitious eye,
> Mervinia for her hills, as for their matchless crowds,
> The nearest that are said to kiss the wand'ring clouds,
> Especial audience craves."

Then, lightly touching the military annals of this shire and the
refuge which her hill-fortresses gave to Welsh patriots, he adds—

> " Her mountains did relieve
> Those whom devouring war else everywhere did grieve."

And then, returning to her general characteristics, he sums up her
honour in the following lines :—

> " And as each one is praised for her peculiar things,
> So only she is rich in mountains, meres, and springs,
> And holds herself as great in her superfluous waste
> As others by their towns and fruitful tillage grac'd."

These passages of the "Polyolbion," though quaint, are very forcible;
and they give a correct impression of the mountain shire within
which the Dee takes its rise.

But in Alpine scenery the mountain and the lake are always
rivals in regard to the expressiveness which they communicate to
the surrounding view. And when Drayton has continued in the
same strain for some space, and has given full emphasis to the boast
of the mountain-nymphs, he introduces the water-nymphs, "Lin-

Tegid that frequent," as exclaiming with indignant jealousy, on behalf of the honour of their lake—

> " What mountain is there found
> In all your monstrous kind (seek ye the island round)
> That truly of himself such wonders can report,
> As can this spacious Lin, the place of our resort ? "

And then these water-nymphs proceed to specify that marvellous peculiarity of their lake and river, which finds a frequent place in the early and unscientific accounts of the Dee. The river, " by his complexion prov'd," glides through the Mere "unmix'd," as the poet says also in his Tenth Song. And, in the passage immediately before us, one result of this strange phenomenon is adduced in respect of the characteristic fish of the lake and the river :—

> " Her wealth again from his she likewise doth divide :
> Those white-fish that in her do wondrously abound,
> Are never seen in him ; nor are his salmons found
> At any time in her."

This curious fancy regarding rivers which pass through lakes has prevailed in many instances. Thus Pliny says, in his " Natural History," that the Rhone flows unmingled through the Lake of Geneva, and the Mincio through the Lago di Garda. Of course, this is a delusion, at which the modern scientific world would smile. And yet there seems to be a fact which might easily suggest to the poetic imagination that the Dee, proudly conscious already of his separate existence, does not deign to unite his waters with those of the lake through which he passes. There is in the lake a peculiar white fish, called the *Gwyniaid*, which is not found in the river; and, conversely, it is said that the salmon—which, as we shall see hereafter, is eminently characteristic of the river—is never caught in the lake. The true explanation is probably that given by Pennant, who, whether as a Naturalist or an Antiquarian, must always be held in honour for his shrewd observation. It does not suit the habits of the salmon to come up farther from the sea than this point, where the Dee flows out of Bala Lake, while the *Gwyniaid* itself is essentially a lake fish. To quote Pennant's own sentence, "the salmon comes in plenty to this place; but neither do they trespass into the lake, and the *Gwyniaid* very rarely into the river."

But now, important as is this lake of Bala, in being the most marked feature of the early course of the Dee, it must be carefully remembered that the lake is not really the fountain of the Dee. There are writers, indeed, who assert that the river does not acquire its name at any higher point than that where it issues from this lake. But this assertion is not in harmony either with the physical facts of the case, or with the traditions and the language of the country people on the spot. The streams which flow into the Mere are so well defined, that one of them must necessarily be the Dee; and the true Dee is the middle one of three such streams, and rises in some low wet ground

Outlet of Bala Lake.

near the road to Dolgelly, two tributaries of greater length than itself flowing in below, one on the right bank from the Arran mountains, the other on the left.

The earliest tributaries of a distinguished river ought by no means to be disregarded, if it were only for the contrasts which their bare and lonely scenery presents, with the well-cultivated and busy places touched by their waters at a later period. But, besides this, these early tributaries themselves have their own spots of extreme

beauty; while there is commonly some grandeur in the hills and
moors around them. Of the two just-mentioned affluents of the Dee,
the Twrch, which rises at the base of Arran Pen Llin, flows through
ravines well worthy of the pedestrian's research. Of the other, the
Lliew, which entices him upwards, though a longer distance, into

On the Dee above Bala.

the heart of the mountains opposite, the writer has a very vivid
recollection. It was early in the year. In fact, the first swallow
had that day been seen in the street of Bala. There had just been
unusually severe weather in all the upper parts of this valley, so that
fears were entertained for the safety of the lambs; and the snow was
cold and crisp on the brown grass, as two ramblers walked from

knoll to knoll, and from waterfall to waterfall, scaring the sheep. But the worst of the weather had now passed away; and in the primroses by the side of the stream, and in the just-opening leaves of the dwarf mountain-ash, though winter was reluctantly departing, there was a delightful and unmistakable " dream of spring."

The interest of the Dee itself, at its source, is of a different kind. It has been implied that there is nothing to recommend it, as regards grandeur or picturesque beauty. Here it is, however, that " the Muses' best pupil, the noble Spenser," as Selden calls the author of the " Faërie Queene," places the home of the childhood of King Arthur. We need not enter here into the details of the legend, or say anything of Vortigern, or of the fortress at the northern edge of Merionethshire, near the head waters of the Conway. The point of importance to us is that here, at the source of the Dee, is the home of old Timon, where he was visited by Merlin, and where the infant king was committed to his care :—

> " His dwelling is low in a valley greene,
> Under the foot of Rauran mossy hore,
> From whence the river Dee, as silver clene,
> His tombling billows rolls with gentle rore."

Whether Spenser ever actually visited this spot it is impossible absolutely to ascertain ; but it is a high satisfaction to the poetic mind to observe that associations of the most venerable and mysterious antiquity are connected with this " wizard stream," even at its origin.

The three brooks (for they are not yet much more than brooks) meet together not far from the small village of Llanwchllyn, which is about a mile above the head of the lake ; and it would be unjust and ungrateful not to add that this hamlet has, in various particulars, a charm of its own—in the moss-grown boulders heaped together by the side of the stream—in the yews which give expression to the little churchyard—in the ruddy beauty of the children—in the comical creature called the " Goat," which is the sign of the tiny

C

hostelry, where oatcake and milk by the fireside are very welcome after a wet walk over the upland pastures in this cold season.

But now we are on the low alluvial ground, where this smooth expanse of water begins ; and a few more words must in this place be given to Bala Lake itself.

Llanwchllyn Village.

Two names of the lake, as was remarked above, are Lin-Tegid and Pimblemere. Of the former term no certain explanation has, so far as I know, ever been given. Tegid has been supposed to be some early Welsh hero, a conjecture which probably indicates that our ignorance on this subject is complete. The word Pimblemere denotes "the lake of the five parishes." To compare small things

with great, we may be reminded here of the Lake of the Four
Cantons in Switzerland. The church of one of these parishes is in
the above-mentioned hamlet : another is marked by a yew-tree on
the south-eastern shore, where a pretty streamlet, flowing over
stones, brings its small contribution to the lake and the Dee :
another, which must be again referred to presently, is marked by
several yews, on the opposite shore, near to the town of Bala. The

size of the lake is about four
miles and a half in length, by
about one mile in breadth. Its
general aspect is quiet and
somewhat desolate. Few boats
are seen on its surface. Its
fishing-rights once belonged to
Basingwerk Abbey, a Cistercian
house which will come before our
notice when we have followed
our river to its entering on the
sea. Now they are the property
of Sir Watkin Williams Wynn,
the great land - owner, whose
name is impressed on all this
region, and one of whose houses
· is seen here, among its woods on
the western edge of the lake.

Old Bridge over the Dee—Llanwchllyn.

But before we leave this sheet
of water, we must notice two of its associations—one scientific, and
the other poetical—which possess a permanent interest.

It might, at first sight, seem absurd to compare the Dee with the
St. Lawrence or the Nile ; but, from our present point of view, the
comparison is perfectly accurate. When a river passes through a
lake, or a system of lakes, the waters of which bear a considerable
proportion in volume to the flow of the stream itself, the river

C 2

acquires from this fact certain features of great importance and utility. The St. Lawrence in Canada, though it flows for hundreds of miles in imposing breadth, is a much less considerable stream than is commonly supposed. Through the whole distance from the lake of the Thousand Islands to Three Rivers (with the exception of the narrow and tortuous channel) it is only a few feet deep; and, but for the vast lakes at its head, it would only be a narrow brook, running in August through parched meadows. The Nile is a river that illustrates the point in hand still more forcibly. We know the confirmation that has been given to the shrewd guess of Ptolemy, that a river which overflows its banks in a dry climate, where it runs for seven hundred miles without a tributary, must have some great reservoir. Were it not for the great reservoir of Bala Lake, the Dee would be almost dry in some seasons. This lake is an instance of what (in the language of the modern engineering world) "catchment powers" can do; for even in a dry summer, when the Dee is just sparkling in a scanty stream over pebbles, a strong south-westerly wind on the Mere will bring on a freshet. Thus the need of giving an adequate water-supply to our great and growing towns in Cheshire and Lancashire has turned the attention of engineers to this lake, and its associated river; and, with this end in view, they were surveyed in the year 1866. Of the general results of the inquiry, it is enough to say here, that by building a breakwater a few feet

Glan-y-llynn : Sir W. W. Wynn's Shooting Box.

high at the narrow outlet of the lake, so as slightly to raise its general surface by damming up a few mountain-passes where the land is of little value, so as in dry summers to store up the water still further in artificial lakes, and by "impounding" the tributary called the Tryweryn, which enters the Dee just below Bala Lake, and which has a very extensive drainage-area,—by these methods it

Bala.

has been calculated that both Liverpool and Manchester might receive a steady supply of water, for all future years, from the Merionethshire hills. These facts or theories are of extreme interest; and the time may soon come when they will be made the subject of renewed consideration.

But—to turn from Science to Poetry—all writers on Bala Lake

have spoken of the sudden flooding of its waters at the outlet under
the influence of a south-west wind ; and this circumstance has been
turned to good account by our present Poet Laureate in one of the
" Idylls of the King."   It is believed that some part of these Idylls
was composed in this immediate neighbourhood, which, as we have
seen, a still earlier poet has associated with the legend of King
Arthur.   However this may be, it would be an unpardonable
omission in this place not to quote the following lines, which speak
of Enid's gentle care of the wounded Geraint :—

> " Her constant motion round him, and the breath
> Of her sweet tendance hovering over him,
> Fill'd all the genial courses of his blood
> With deeper and with ever deeper love,
> As the south-west that blowing Bala Lake
> Fills all the sacred Dee."

With this quotation we may pass from the lake to the little town
which stands near the outflow of the river.

Of the town of Bala itself, it must be admitted that on a cold
and drizzling day (and such days in Wales are perhaps not infre-
quent) it is as dull and dreary a place as can well be imagined. Not
so, however, when the sun shines on its gray houses and the distant
prospect : and to the honour of the little town it must be added that
it has trees in its modest street, and thus possesses one element of
beauty, which belongs to nearly every foreign town, but which we,
with British obstinacy, for the most part discard.

In the views around Bala, two objects may be singled out, one
belonging to Nature which does not change, the other to a very
modern passage of changing human history.

It would be rash to say that every lake has its own peculiar
mountain. But in the case of many lakes this connection is found,
and it is always very full of expression. The reader will know what
is meant, if he has ever gazed on Skiddaw from a boat on the bright
surface of Derwentwater, or watched from the foot of Loch Lomond

the great shoulders of Ben Lomond darkening in the evening sky. In the instance before us the mountain does not exercise so towering a command over the lake; but still, it is with true geographical propriety that Arran Pen Llin—"Mighty Raran," as Drayton terms it—derives its name from the lake in combination with which it is

Llanycil Church.

seen to so much advantage from many spots near the town of Bala ; and perhaps no better place is to be found for this characteristic view than among the yew-trees in the little churchyard of Llanycil. But a modest tomb in this churchyard carries our thoughts to the other view which was referred to above.

We must take one more glance at the surrounding hills before

we descend the river by Corwen to Llangollen; and this time we
turn our eyes towards the Arenig mountains on the right, from
whence the Tryweryn flows to the low flat meadows, through which,
at last, it passes in many windings to the Dee below the town of
Bala. This view is embellished and diversified by a handsome range

Llanycil, from South Side.

of buildings, beyond the level fields, and with a background of hills.
The buildings are those of a Divinity College, for the training of
Nonconformist Ministers; nor could any place be more fitly chosen
for such an institution. For Charles of Bala, whose grave in
Llanycil churchyard has been mentioned, was a prominent figure in
a chapter of Church history, which remains yet unwritten, and which

if details of scenery were duly combined with those of biography, might easily be made singularly attractive. It is not to be expected that an English Churchman can write with enthusiasm of the annals of Nonconformity; but it was in connection with the services of the Church of England, and in harmony with her doctrines, that the movement began, of which Charles of Bala is the representative; and his Welsh Theological Dictionary, and his efforts for the diffusion and study of the Bible, as well as his whole career, show that he was no fanatic, but an eminently wise and laborious, as well as godly and devoted man.

At this point we quit the Alpine region — properly so called—of the river Dee; and there is an obvious temptation here to pause on the characteristics of the mountain-scenery of Wales as compared with that of the Scottish Highlands, or of Cumberland and Westmoreland. It is very difficult, however, accurately to describe such differences, though we may be very con-

Pont Cennant.

scious of their reality. The Cambrian district of our island is strongly contrasted with the Cumbrian by the fact that the latter has a multitude of lakes, the former hardly any; and, in fact, we have in this chapter been occupied with the only marked exception to the rule. In the Highlands, the features generally are grander and larger; and the mist is certainly heavier and thicker. Perhaps the most peculiar charm of Welsh mountain-scenery consists in the tenderness of its atmospheric effects. This is written under the recollection of "a troubled day with broken lights" at Bala, when the rain was like a veil of faint violet, through which sunlight was seen gently resting on green woods and distant hills.

Bala Lake at one time abounded with fine trout; but, unfortunately, pike were introduced by an owner of Wynnestay some years ago, and trout are scarce. Very fine perch abound, and an effort is being made to introduce the American black bass, a fish of the perch tribe, but much finer in every way, and affording the most excellent sport to the angler. That these fish will take kindly to the waters there cannot be a doubt, as the conditions of the lake and the rivers that flow into it and out are precisely similar to those in America, where these fish are in their primest condition. A reciprocal return will be made with the English sole, a fish that once abounded in the estuary of the Dee, and is yet frequently met with, but a fish that is not known in America.

III.

OWEN GLENDOWER.

DIFFICULTY OF COMBINING THE COURSE OF THE RIVER CONSECUTIVELY WITH THE
COURSE OF HISTORY—SCENERY OF THIS PART OF THE DEE—LLANDERFEL—CORWEN—
CAREER AND CHARACTER OF OWEN GLENDOWER—SURVIVING MEMORIALS OF HIM—
LLANTISILIO — LLANGOLLEN — VALLE CRUCIS ABBEY — THE CISTERCIANS AND ST.
BERNARD — FOUNDING OF THIS MONASTERY — THE RUINS — DECAY OF THE SEVERE
MONASTIC SPIRIT.

N combining the description of a river with notices of biographical or national events, it is not possible either to follow the stream continuously without sometimes breaking the thread of the history, or to pursue the sequence of the history without sometimes retracing our steps along the banks of the stream. We must take our choice between one method or the other. Either we must select the river as our guide, gathering up, as we proceed, the history on as orderly a system as we can ; or else, pursuing historical and biographical annals consecutively, we must press the river into our service here and there, in its bright open reaches and its long windings, just as we use pictures to illustrate a book. In the present instance the former plan is evidently that which we are called upon to adopt. Our main subject is not the history of the north-eastern borderland of England and Wales, but the description of the river Dee.

The geographical extent of country now immediately before our thoughts is defined by the course of the Dee from Bala to Llangollen.

This part of our journey takes us over the region which is especially
famous in the annals of Wales as the native ground of Owen Glendower; and bringing us, as it does, at the close, to the charming
ruins of Valle Crucis Abbey, it invites us to include in this chapter
some notices of that abbey, and of the Cistercians by whom it was
founded.

The scenery in the range of country to which this portion of the
Dee belongs is of extreme beauty throughout. In fact, it is the
most beautiful scenery with which we shall have to deal in the whole
of this our task of observing and noting down the features of this
stream. At the same time there is great variety even in the limited
space that is under our present attention. Two general facts may
be mentioned here: first, that the Berwyn mountains are on our
right all the way; and, secondly, that the river, though it has its
" pauses of reluctant pride," falls very considerably from Bala to
Llangollen.

When we leave Bala and pass the point where the large tributary
above mentioned, the Tryweryn, having "taken his stream" "from
a native lin" among the Arenig mountains—

> " Out of Pimblemere where Dee himself doth win,
>   Along with him his lord full constantly doth glide,"

other smaller affluents meanwhile preparing (still to quote Drayton) —

> " Their Dee into the bounds of Denbigh to convey,"

we find the open watery meadows contracting somewhat suddenly
into a gorge of exquisite beauty, where the river runs winding
between deep banks covered with trees. In the heart of all this
delightful scene is the village of Llanderfel, where a picturesque
bridge crosses the stream, and where bare rocky hill-tops add just
the requisite touch of severity to the warm gentle foliage by the
sparkling water, to say nothing of the grotesque legends which give
to the spot a charm of their own. We are here in the celebrated

vale of Edeyrnion; and well is the pedestrian rewarded, who explores this valley leisurely, along the fishermen's paths by the river-side, and the high slopes of the hills above. Nor are the reminiscences of Welsh heroism wanting here for those who wish to combine in their thoughts History with Nature. It is on one of these heights that the "bloody brow" is pointed out where the father of many sons, who had died fighting against the Saxons, said to the last survivor:— "Defend the brow of yonder hill: be the event what it may, when there is but one son left, it is vain to be too fond of him."

After this gorge is left behind, the valley of the Dee widens out again into open spaces, which are comparatively bare and even bleak. The course of a river is like the course of human life, in which there often occurs at an early period some broad quiet level, where the retrospect of the days just preceding is lively and delightful, while the present is somewhat wanting in points of interest and variety. We must not, however, be unjust to this particular region of the Dee. Though not comparable to that which immediately precedes or that which immediately follows, it abounds in charming subjects for the artist, whether he chooses for his pencil the cattle which stand in the quiet places of the stream, or the sycamores and alders that fringe it where it runs more rapidly, or whether, looking away from the river, he sees how pictures are suggested to him again and again, by larches intermingling with fragments of rock.

The great interest, however, of this region is that it is Owen Glendower's country, the little town of Corwen being the central point. Here, then, is the place to pause for a moment on the life and career of this remarkable man. It is impossible not to feel, with a shade of disappointment, that if Wales had ever possessed a Sir Walter Scott, we should have known far more concerning Owen Glendower than we do know, or, at least, that he would have stood out with lineaments more definitely marked on the canvas of Fiction. It is remarkable that we seem to have no record of his personal appearance, his customary gestures or phrases, or the colour of his eyes and hair. The only circumstance of this kind on record is one which is noted on an occasion when for a moment his brother's dead body was supposed to be the corpse of the prince himself, and when the mistake was speedily corrected by observing that in this case there was no wart above the eyebrow. Still Glendower is very well known to us, and very well worthy of remembrance; and nowhere do we become more conscious of this than when we think of him in connection with his own proper home on the banks of the Dee.

The period of Glendower's conspicuous career is given to us most definitely, not merely by a general recurrence to the great events of the time, but by the most exact chronology. The first year of the fifteenth century marks it out for us with the utmost precision; and it is remarkable that we have the help of topography too, in the transactions at Flint Castle, on this very river Dee, to which allusion will be made hereafter. There is no space here for more than a bare enumeration of the general facts of Glendower's active life: his early education in London as a barrister-at-law; his high and honourable position as a military officer under Richard II.; the seizure, immediately on the accession of Henry IV., by Lord Gray of Ruthin, of a tract of land to which Glendower laid claim; the unfair method by which he was discredited at the court; the warning of the Bishop of St. Asaph, in the House of Lords, that if some redress were not found, danger was imminent, to which some of the lords replied "that they did not fear that rascally bare-footed people;" the steps by which Glendower's enthusiastic mind was led to rally the spirit of Welsh independence against the English king; the frequent and unsuccessful attempts to subdue him among the fastnesses of his native mountains; the treaties he signed, as though an independent monarch, with the King of France; then his disasters, his wanderings, his sheltering in caves; and finally his obscure death, with a legacy of difficult circumstances and oppressive laws left behind in Wales. Of course, Glendower is called a rebel and a traitor. But Henry IV. was successful, Glendower was not; and, if we blame this outburst of local nationality, at least we are bound to remember that only a century had then passed since Edward I. had brought the Welsh into real subjection to the English Crown.

As to his character, a greater master than Scott has placed "the irregular and wild Glendower" before us with remarkable distinctness, and made us to know that he was "not in the roll of common men." Especially we must mark the poetic temperament which led him readily to believe that he was "the heir of prophecy." An old historian puts the matter thus : — "His good success over Lord Gray, together with the numerous resort of the Welsh to him, and the favourable interpretation of the predictions of Merlin, which some construed very advantageously, made the swelling mind of Glendower overflow its banks, and gave him a hope of

Owen Glendower's Prison.

restoring this island back to the Britons." The popular estimate of Glendower seems everywhere to have surrounded him with circumstances of wonder. Marvellous sights and sounds were seen and heard in the heavens at his birth ; and when the English troops were defeated it was thought (to quote the same author) that the Welsh chieftain "through art magike caused such foule weather of winde, tempeste, raine, snow, and haile, to be raised

for the annoiance of the king's armie, that the like had not been hearde of."

Various relics of Glendower have been preserved in his native neighbourhood. Some of them appear to have been recently dispersed. Those, however, which are here represented seem to be

Owen Glendower's Mound.

authentic. Near " Owen Glendower's Mound," which commands a most beautiful view of the river Dee, is an old farm-house containing a table of large size, which from time immemorial has been called "Owen Glendower's Table." Other remains are political rather than domestic, and are found at Dolgelly. The "Parliament House," where a treaty with France is said to have been signed, is still shown ; and its oak-roof and oak-carvings correspond in appearance with the characteristic wood-work of the early part of the fifteenth century, which we find in various parts of England.

One memorial, however, of Glendower, and that the best, survives, without any risk of change, in the scenery of his native region. The compara-tively open character of that part of the valley of the Dee, of which Corwen is the small cen-

Owen Glendower's Table.

tral town, has been mentioned above. We must now pass on to a part of its course where this valley contracts again, and where rich woods close in upon the windings of the river. To the traveller by railway a tunnel marks the transition from Merionethshire to Denbighshire. The river is immediately below. Telford's famous coach - road passes higher up the hill on the same side, commanding exquisite views. We are often in the habit of finding fault with railways as being enemies to our enjoyment of the pic-turesque : but a railway-tunnel is sometimes the cold and gloomy prelude to a scene of cheerful beauty, admired all the

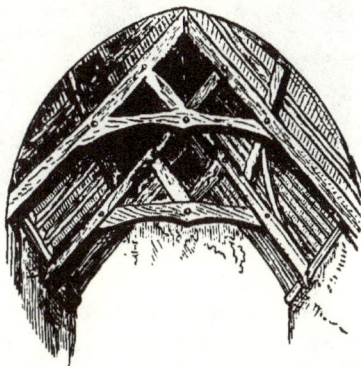

Oak Roof at Dolgelly.

more because the sight of it is accompanied with a start of surprise. So it is, in some degree, at this place. Few spots in this island are

D

more lovely than the reach of the river Dee near Llantisilio, as
seen, for instance, in the late summer, when the trees are in their
richest foliage, and when, beyond the level meadow opposite, the
thick beds of foxglove on the distant hills produce a warm glow
of colouring brighter than heather.

The Parliament House, Dolgelly.

And now we are in the deep hollow of the exquisite Vale of Llangollen. Much has been written on the beauty of this valley, and of
the valleys which open out of it; and nowhere has more been written
on this subject, or more pleasantly, than in the popular guide-books
for tourists. For this very reason, and also because our limits are
restricted, we may be excused for giving a very scanty space to

the objects worthy of regard in this famous part of the course of the Dee.

The story of the "Two Ladies of Llangollen" we may leave in the pages of Madame de Genlis, where it has found a most appropriate place. The bridge, which is well worthy of careful

Valley Farm, near Corwen.

notice, both on account of its history, and in connection with the broad flat rock on which it stands, must be deferred to that chapter, in which the various bridges and ferries of the Dee will be discussed in their association with human affairs. We must leave to the geologists the huge, bare escarpment of the Eglwyseg limestone rocks, which form so grand a background to some of the views in this

neighbourhood. Even Castle Dinas Bran must be passed by with
a very slight notice. This seems the more unfair, because the Dee
is not, like some rivers, wealthy in the ruins of ancient castles.
The only two instances, in fact, are this and the Castle of Flint.
Moreover, the hill of Dinas Bran asserts its claim on our attention,
because it is bold and conspicuous in the general view of Llangollen.

In the Vale of Llangollen.

It has also its appropriate romance in the love of a great lady of
the house of Tudor Trevor, and of a lowly bard who wrote Welsh
poetry in her honour. The remains of the Castle, which were
once considerable, are fast mouldering away, and in their present
aspect they remind us of Kendal Castle; though with this difference between the two ruins, that the latter has the recollection
of Catherine Parr to connect it definitely with a critical time of

English history, the former seems destitute of any noted reminiscence of the past.

There is, however, one ruin near Llangollen, on which we must pause somewhat longer. This is Valle Crucis Abbey. Two Cistercian houses have an important connection with the aspect and the history of the Dee. One of them has been mentioned above, and will be mentioned again. But Valle Crucis possesses far greater interest than Basingwerk. Both, however, deserve our most careful attention. No religious order of the Middle Ages is more attractive than that of the Cistercians; and on none has the imagination so good an opportunity of dwelling in the midst of beautiful scenery. Other monastic orders, both on their picturesque and on their learned side, will come before our notice when we reach the city of Chester. This order belongs peculiarly to the country. Whenever we are among the ruins of Cistercian Abbeys, we may always expect

Llangollen, looking over Dee Bridge.

the appearance of nature around to be pleasing and attractive; and this for two reasons. The austere motives which inspired their foundation led to the choice of wild and secluded places. " Believe me," said St. Bernard, " I have learnt more from trees than ever I learnt from men." But further, the work of these monks having been chiefly agricultural, they gradually brought the solitudes which delighted them into a gentler beauty, and thus they left near their ruined homes a charm in the aspect of nature greater than that which they found.

The impulse given throughout Europe in the twelfth century to monastic life from that part of France where Citeaux was founded on the borders of Burgundy and Champagne, was most remarkable.

Eglwyseg Rocks.

The greatest name connected with the Cistercians is, of course, that of Bernard of Clairvaux. He, in fact, during his life, ruled both the intellect and the politics of Europe, to say nothing of the Crusades. Still, the true founder of this particular branch of the Benedictines was Stephen Harding, an Englishman ; and England can boast of a full share of beautiful abbeys connected with these two historic names. It is to be remembered, too, that the church architecture of the early part of the thirteenth century is admirable in its simplicity, dignity, and grace.

Valle Crucis Abbey, indeed, is not to be compared with the great Cistercian houses of Yorkshire—Rivaulx, Byland, Fountains, Kirkstall, and Jervaux—and yet it wears the impress of its time architecturally, as well as in the characteristic seclusion and beauty of its position.

It was exactly in the year 1200 that Madoc, Lord of Bromfield, at the time when Prince Llewellyn was contending with King John, founding this monastic house in a deep hollow, already called the Valley of the Cross, from a monumental cross which stood there previously, and stands there still, under the name of Eliseg's Pillar. The hills all round are remarkably steep, so that some excuse is afforded for the following comical account of the position of the Abbey. The lines are by Churchyard, a poet of the reign of Queen Elizabeth, whose chief claim on our attention resides in the quaintness of his style and spelling. But perhaps three hundred years hence our own mode of writing will seem as strange to those who come after us as this does to us now :—

Castle Dinas Bran.

> " An abbey nere that mountayne town there is,
> Whose walles yet stand, and steeple too likewise ;
> But who that rides to see the troth of this,
> Shall thinke he mounts on hilles unto the skyes ;
> For when one hill behind your backe you see,
> Another comes, two tymes as hye as hee :
> And in one place the mountaynes stand so there
> In roundnesse such, as it a cockpit were."

From these lines it would appear that the central tower was then standing ; and the piers show that such a tower was a part of the original design. Now it has entirely disappeared. And twenty years ago heaps of rubbish and the bold and reckless growth of trees had greatly obscured the other features of the church. About that

time excavations and clearing were begun in earnest; and quite
recently steps have been taken, in excellent taste, to arrest the
progress of further decay, so that the characteristic forms of the
abbey can be examined and admired without discomfort. The conventual buildings, indeed, on the south of the church, have been
turned into farm buildings: and it is difficult to discriminate their

Remains of Valle Crucis Abbey.

exact arrangement, though several portions of great interest remain.
But the eastern and western ends of the church, rising boldly up to
their pointed gables, are fine objects in the landscape; and the
character of their architecture is sufficiently distinctive to attract
separate attention. The manner in which, at the east end, the flat
buttresses spread themselves, as it were, round the lancet windows is

very curious, while the west end is stated, on high authority, to connect itself with a certain recognised type of North Welsh archi-

Valle Crucis : West Gable of Abbey Church.

tecture, as Llandaff and St. David's Cathedrals are said to be allied to the contemporary buildings of South-Western England.

In the days of Owen Glendower the prosperity of this religious

house was probably at its height, with its sense of security undisturbed, and with nothing to predict that in a hundred and fifty years
the havoc of its destruction would be complete. And yet this decay
was, at that very time, beginning with the luxury and pomp which
had invaded even the Cistercians. Valle Crucis Abbey, at this
period, was an establishment of no inconsiderable importance. One

Remains of Valle Crucis Abbey.

of its abbots was selected by King Henry VII. to aid in drawing
out his Welsh pedigree ; and soon afterwards two others were made
in succession Bishops of St. Asaph. Another abbot of about the
same period is the subject of the panegyric of two Welsh poets.
He is called "the pope of the glen"—in his "white frock" sur-
passing all other abbots. His entertainments are "like the leaves

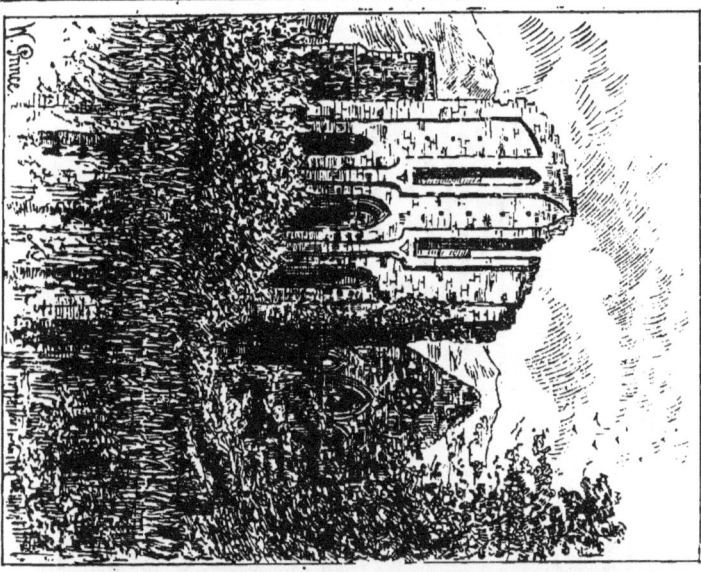

THE ARBITRATOR'S AWARD IN THE CARPENTERS' DISPUTE.

NO INCREASE OF PAY, BUT REDUCTION OF WORKING HOURS, AND ADVANCED PAY FOR OVERTIME.

THE arbitrator, Mr. J. MacVicar Anderson, F.R.I.B.A., in the matters in dispute between the Central Association of Master Builders and the carpenters and joiners of London, issued his award at noon yesterday (Thursday). The document narrates at considerable length, and in some detail, the steps which had led up to the arbitration, giving the eight points of the memorial presented to the Central Master Builders' Association by the United Trades Committee of Carpenters and Joiners, which were, in effect, a demand for (1) a reduction of working time from 52½ to 47 hours per week, (2) an advance of wages from 9d. to 10d. per hour, (3) increase of pay for overtime, (4) an allowance for expenses to men sent to a distance from the shop or job, (5) the abolition of subletting and piece-work, (6) the providing in shops and on jobs of a lock-up place for tools, (7) of a place for meals, and (8) one hour's notice and one hour's wages for grinding to be allowed on discharge. These amended rules were, if conceded, to have come into force on May 2; but being refused by the master builders, a partial strike against three representative firms took place, replied to on May 23 by a general lock-out. A compromise was offered by the employers on the 27th July, but, being declined, was withdrawn

and one hour to be allowed for dinner on each of the first five working days of the week, except in the depth of winter, when half an hour only is allowed. The sixteen weeks of winter are to be reckoned eight on each side of Christmas-day.

2. The standard rate of wages in shops and on jobs to be 9d. per hour.

3. Overtime, when worked at the request of the employer, but not otherwise, to be paid at the following rates per hour:—From 5.15 p.m. in summer, and 5 p.m. in winter until 8 p.m., one shilling per hour; from 8 p.m. until 10 p.m., one shilling and threepence per hour; from 10 p.m. till the time of starting next morning, one shilling and sixpence per hour. On Saturdays, from 12 noon until 4 p.m., one shilling per hour, and from 4 p.m. till the time of starting on Monday, one shilling and sixpence per hour. No overtime to be reckoned until the full working day has been made.

4. Men who are sent from the shop to a job, including those sent into the country, shall be allowed as expenses one shilling per day for any distance over six miles from the shop or job, exclusive of travelling expenses, and allowance for time spent in travel.

5. Employers shall provide a lock-up place on jobs where practicable, and shall take reasonable precautions for securing workmen's tools, but without incurring responsibility in case of loss.

6. Employers shall provide, both in shops and on jobs where practicable and reasonable, some suitable place for the workmen to have their

or asphalte. The author shows the rule of obtaining depth and width of footings and concrete. Thus the area of footings should equal Safe load on concrete. Plates 2, 3, and 4 give varieties of English and Flemish bond, illustrated by large-scale plans of courses for walls at right angles, showing the closers at angle and stopped ends, from one brick to three bricks in thickness. Single Flemish bond, details of brick arches of various forms, chimney showing the arrangement of flues are given, these plates being revised by Mr. H. W. Richards' lecture on brickwork and masonry. The stone walls illustrated give uncoursed random rubble, coursed rubble, irregular course or "snecked", walls, besides squared rubble in courses, block-in-course, and ashlar walls with brick or rubble backing. Joggles, slate and metal cramping, are also indicated. Stone staircases are fully detailed and figured, in which the steps and landings and the rebated back-joints of the steps are shown. Modes of tailing steps supported on walls, joggled landings, and soffits flush and broken are detailed. In the carpentry section plans of single floors showing fireplace, trimming, methods of jointing floor-boards; plans and details of double-framed floors with wood and iron binders appear. Roofs and partitions with details and stress diagrams; a Mansard roof truss for a 30ft. span, with perspective sketches, are useful. Passing joiner's work, which has been revised by Mr. G. C. Pope, and is well done, we present limits will tend to restraint of trade, and to bring disaster on all concerned.

Regarding Clause 3, it is reasonable that over-time should be paid at a higher rate than ordinary labour; but inasmuch as overtime is often necessary, the rate should not be pro-hibitive.

Clause 4 of the memorial has been so amended as to include men sent into the country, and is agreed to.

Clause 5 (prohibitive of sub-letting and piece-work) has not been insisted upon, and I make no rule respecting it.

The remaining three clauses have been practically agreed to, subject to certain modifications, and are embraced in my award.

On and after the date of this award (yesterday) the code of working rules for carpenters and joiners in the London district shall be—

1. The working time, both in shops and on jobs, shall be 51¼ hours per week for 36 weeks in summer, and 47 hours per week for 16 weeks in winter, equal on an average to 50 work-ing hours all the year round. The hour for commencing work to be 6.30 a.m. for the 16 winter weeks, and 7.0 a.m. for the 16 winter weeks. The hour for leaving off work on the first five working days of the week shall be 5.15 p.m. for the 36 summer weeks, and 5 p.m. for the 16 winter weeks, except in the depth of winter on outdoor jobs, when it is to be 4.30 p.m. The hour for leaving off work on Saturdays to be 12 o'clock noon all the year round. Half an hour to be allowed for breakfast every working day,

in the direction aimed at. The principle of the reduction of hours having been conceded, they assert that an upward movement in wages will be forced by the action of the other building trades. The arbitrator's award, however unpalatable to the men in respect to wages, will, however, be loyally submitted to by all parties.

BOOKS RECEIVED.

Forty Plates on Building Construction, by CHARLES F. MITCHELL, M.S.A., M.A.A., Lecturer on Building Construction at the Poly-technic Institute, &c., assisted by the Lecturers of the latter (London: Cassell and Company).—This series of plates, which can be obtained in sets for the different trades, has been prepared to assist students studying for the examina-tions in the elementary, advanced, and honours stages of Building Construction and Drawing of the Science and Art Department, and for the examinations of the City and Guilds of London Institute. They will also be valuable, we think, in offices where pupils are taken, and every architect would do well to have the volume before us. One merit of the drawings is that every part and detail is figured. Mr. Mitchell has been assisted by his colleagues at the Institute at which he is lecturer. The details given of brickwork show isometrical drawings of piers from one brick to three bricks, and their foot-ings; every alternate course of bond is clearly shown, also the dump-course of hygeian rock

switch-boards; also the out-of-door structures, such as standards for carrying the wires, trussed standards and arms, means for regulating the sag of the wires, and the systems in use known as the "twist," and "cross" systems for arranging the wires. The student of electrical appliances will find much general information on the theory and history of the subject of telephony in this little work.

Councillor J. R. Corby, architect, Stamford, was on the 4th inst. duly elected a Fellow of the Sur-veyors' Institution.

A Methodist New Connexion Sunday-school a Deighton, near Huddersfield, was opened on Thurs-day in last week. It provides in the assembly-hall seats for 400 scholars; in addition there are five classrooms. Mr. J. Brooke, of Hindley, executed the masonry, and Mr. D. Light, of Cowcliffe, the joinery.

To celebrate the opening of the new free reading-room at the Hampstead public library, a conversa-zione was held on Wednesday week at the library, Stanfield House, High-street. The room has been erected as a memorial, and was built by Messrs. Burford and Son, of High-street, from the designs of Mr. Horace Field, of Church-row, Hampstead.

Messrs. E. Miller and Co., Limited, Leeds, have had placed in front of their premises at the bottom of New Briggate, near the public dispensary, Leeds, a large illuminated clock, made and fixed by Messrs. Wm. Potts and Sons, clock manufacturers, Guildford-street and Cookridge-street, Leeds, makers of the Royal Exchange, Thornton Arcade, and New Arcade clocks, Leeds.

in summer." There is " vocal and instrumental music " at dinner in Valle Crucis. The wine, the ale, and the various dishes make the feast " like a carnival." The guests have " a thousand apples for dessert." The change is evidently great since the time when the early Cistercians adopted the white cassock as a badge of the severity of their rule, in contrast to the self-indulgence associated with the dark costume of other branches of the great and varied family of Benedictine monks.

IV.

THE BRITONS AND SAXONS ON THE DEE.

DESCENT OF THE RIVER FROM LLANGOLLEN—NORTH WALES COAL-FIELD—JUNCTION OF THE CEIRIOG AND THE DEE—AQUEDUCTS AND VIADUCTS—OFFA'S DYKE AND WATT'S DYKE—FRESCO IN RUABON CHURCH—THE BORDER OF SHROPSHIRE—DETACHED PART OF FLINTSHIRE—OVERTON—CORACLES—BANGOR MONACHORUM—PELAGIUS—THE HALLELUJAH VICTORY—INTERVIEW WITH AUGUSTINE—MASSACRE OF THE MONKS—ENTRANCE INTO CHESHIRE.

UR last glimpse of history in connection with the Dee related to a period definite and distinct. The military figures before our thoughts were the soldiers of King Henry IV., with their plate-armour, which had then taken the place of the chain-armour of an earlier period, and the brave irregular troops of Owen Glendower, with whatever picturesque combination of defensive or tattered attire they were able to command. The men of peace, so far as they were men of peace, were the Cistercians of Valle Crucis, gossiping with the market-people of Llangollen, or engaged in the austere and devout duties of their monastery; for assuredly characters of both kinds were abundantly found among the inmates of that religious house.

We must now, as we enter upon the next selected portion of the river, prepare for very varied passages, both of scenery and history. The Dee will now become both a Welsh stream and an English stream. Sloping banks will be combined in our view, through many windings, with wide-spread plains. We shall pass rapidly through one district which is dusty and dingy with industrial work. We shall be close within reach of grand and princely residences, full of the memories of feudal times, of the wars of the Commonwealth, and of the early continental struggles of this present century. We shall be arrested by those triumphs of engineering which belong to this last period. Salmon-fishing and ecclesiastical controversy are among the topics which will force themselves on our attention. We must ask the friendly Dee to bind all these things together for us in its continuous progress from Castle Dinas Bran to Holt and Farndon Bridge. Meanwhile, as we lightly touch these several topics, we are to bear in mind that one great historical subject is chiefly before our thoughts in this section of our task. The conflict of the Saxons and Britons in England can in no district of the country be studied with an easier or more lively association with physical features, than in this part of the course of the Dee. By keeping this combination carefully in view we shall be consistent both with poetry and with fact.

Quitting now Llangollen, and after taking a last look at those houses perched high on steep hill-sides, which give to this place part of its distinctive character, we pass along a somewhat contracted valley, well worthy of being explored on foot and at leisure by the immediate banks of the stream. But, if we are travelling by railway, we find ourselves very speedily in the midst of that disfigurement of fine scenery, which is the inevitable result of collieries and ironworks. It is difficult now to believe how beautiful the country once was in the immediate neighbourhood of such towns as Leeds and Stockport and Manchester. Something of the same kind of change has taken place in that part of the course of the Dee where it crosses the North Wales coal-field. This condition of things, however, does not continue over a large space. For a moment our eye is distressed by the sight of squalid houses, and of a rough and discoloured, though probably thriving, population;

but presently we have before us brighter and more attractive aspects of the banks of our stream.

From Trevor station, which is placed just where the river leaves the sub-Alpine country, and prepares to enter upon those plains and low undulating hills which, whether English or not in name, have all the English characteristics, a view is obtained of certain grand engineering and architectural works, to which our attention must afterwards be given in detail. At present we only glance at their general effect—and this is certainly very striking. It would be a great mistake to say that a well-marked horizontal line, or a long series of arches, is of necessity hostile to the beauty of a landscape. What we all acknowledge in regard to the aqueducts of the Roman Campagna, this—after making due allowance for the charm of colour which is due to time and ruin, and the charm of mystery which belongs to old history as opposed to the business and bustle of the present—we must in justice acknowledge on behalf of those aqueducts and viaducts which cross the country near the meeting of the Ceiriog and the Dee.

Across the ground which is grandly broken and diversified by a projecting spur of the Berwyn hills, between the valleys of these two streams, it is remarkable that engineering works of great importance should have been vigorously thrown, both in the eighth century and the eighteenth. Some mystery still rests upon the origin and true import of "Offa's Dyke" and "Watt's Dyke." It is here, however, that we encounter them at their south-eastern extremity; and we cannot omit to mention them. Moreover, they certainly belong, more or less, to that conflict between the Saxons and Britons, which has been named as the special historical subject of this chapter. We shall be called to notice these same lines of demarcation again, at the north-western extremity, beyond Flint, on the estuary of the Dee. It is enough here to quote the lines of "honest Churchyard, the simple swan of the reign of Elizabeth," as he is called by Pennant, who, indeed, says that this poet was the first to distinguish between the two dykes. He has been speaking of the Ceiriog, " a wonderous violent water, when rayne or snowe is greate," and of the Dee, a "river deepe and swifte," which runs "with gushing streame" to Chester "all along;" and then he adds :—

> "Within two myles there is a famous thing
> Cal'de Offac's Dyke, that reacheth farre in length:
> All kinds of ware the Danes might thither bring:
> It was free ground, and cal'de the Britaines strength.
> Wats Dyke likewise about the same was set,
> Betweene which two both Danes and Britaines met,
> . And trafficke still; but, passing bounds by sleight,
> The one did take the other prisoner streight."

These lines have often been quoted, but usually without the moral, which it is quite worth while to append :—

> "Thus foes could meete (as many tymes they may)
> And doe no harm, when profit ment they both;
> Good rule and lawe make baddest things to stay,
> The els by rage to wretched revell goeth."

The mention of the Danes by this old poet introduces a further complication into a subject already somewhat intricate. But on this we need not now dwell. We shall have occasion to refer to the Danes again when we reach the estuary.

On the right and on the left of this meeting-ground of the Dee and the Ceiriog are the grand feudal castle of Chirk and the palatial residence of Wynnestay, near Ruabon, each with its noble park. These must be deferred to the chapter to which such topics will more particularly belong. A brief pause, however, may be made at Ruabon itself.

In these slight papers, moving, as we do, very rapidly from point to point, we are forced to make a selection among many subjects of attraction; and, in illustration of this place, we must confine ourselves to a fresco which has lately come to view in the process of repairing the south wall of the church. Its date is probably of the fifteenth century, and the figures in the picture, though quaint and stiff, are very full of meaning. It is of considerable size, but the delineation here given of it on a small scale is correct. The subject is a procession representing the deeds of mercy enumerated in the 25th chapter of St. Matthew, and the benediction and the entering into life of those who do such deeds. Certain of the scenes are somewhat dim and obliterated, but "the clothing of the naked" is very distinctly shown. In the "giving of drink to the thirsty" the glass is curiously like the hock glasses in use along the Rhine at the present day. The benediction in each case is expressed by an angel, spreading out his hands in approval. The "Enter thou into the joy of thy Lord" is indicated by figures on an inclined plane to the right; and it seems probable that immediately beneath we have the beginning of another inclined plane, arranged to show in another procession the dread alternative in this solemn passage of Scripture.

Chirk Village.

It should be particularly noticed that about these parts the Dee becomes a border river in more respects than one. From its junction with the Ceiriog for two or three miles, till it approaches Erbistock, it is the boundary of Denbighshire and Shropshire. Here, then, we touch English soil, and yet soil which once was Welsh. The poet Churchyard, who was himself

from Shrewsbury gives us some words here, which we may use
for our purpose—

"Can Wales be named, and Shropshire be forgot?"

And then he says, that while speaking well of all, he must still have
an eye "to native soyle," and that nothing can "goe beyond his
countries love." Yet—"the Worthiness of Wales" being his theme
—he adds, concerning the district which we here touch—

"Wales once it was; and yet, to mend thy tale,
Make Wales the park, and plaine Shropsheare the pale.
If 'pale' be not a speciall peace of parke,
Sit silent now, and neither write nor speake;
But leave our 'pale,' and thou mayst misse the marke
Thy Muse would hit."

Ancient Fresco at Ruabon.

Shropshire, however, can claim but a very small portion of our
space. The Dee presently becomes, most curiously, the boundary
between Flintshire and Denbighshire, a detached portion of the
former county being thrown over the latter, like a great boulder
disjointed from the mountains, so as to interpose a fragment of
Wales between Shropshire and Cheshire. Within this portion of
its course, during which the Dee is again a thoroughly Welsh

E

river, two spots particularly demand our attention—Overton and Bangor.

It is remarkable that of the seven wonders of North Wales four are within the range of that portion of the river which has been marked out for the present chapter, and one only just beyond it. These are, in order, according to the proverbial

Overton Church.

saying, Llangollen bridge, Overton churchyard, Wrexham steeple, and Gresford bells. In the origin and acceptance of this proverb, there is manifest a love of picturesque beauty, as well as a disposition to wonder at the curiosities and triumphs of Art. The neighbourhood of Overton has so much that is lovely and striking in the curves of the river, and in its views of broad levels contrasted with hilly ground, that it will be a great pleasure hereafter to revert to this part of the Dee. At present the old British associations of the river being proposed as a chief subject for the moment, there is a temptation to pause on one reminiscence of the earliest inhabitants of this island, which in this neighbourhood remains very fresh.

Overton Cemetery.

Very few ancient British words survive in our modern English language. One of these is the term "basket," which denoted wicker-work in the oldest time, as it does now. It is interesting to recall this philological fact, when we see in this particular part of the course of the Dee those primitive boats of wicker-work which are named "coracles." This name, indeed, has by some been supposéd to be Latin, and to be derived from the "corium" or hide, that was used to cover the basket-laths of which the boats are made. The covering now is usually of canvas coated with pitch. Each of these boats costs about £2 in the making, weighs about fourteen pounds, and will contain two men. The mode of paddling in these boats is similar to that of the North American Indians, except that the latter paddle on the sides of their canoes. It is obvious that a coracle-race must be amusing. The men who win such races on the lower part of the Dee, at Chester, almost always come from the neighbourhood of Bangor. These boats are useful, not only for ferrying across the river, but for netting salmon. The coracle here represented was so employed at the moment when it was sketched, and a splendid fish of twenty-two pounds, clean from the sea, was the result.

Coracles.

The mention of salmon takes us at once to Bangor, for just above Bangor Bridge is one of the finest spawning-grounds on the Dee. In the view given on p. 54 the church of the village is represented in combination with the bridge. This church would in any case deserve a pause in our progress, because of the historic circumstances mentioned below ; but for its own sake it is worthy of attention. In the lower story of the bell-tower is the following quaint inscription, which it is quite worth while to give, though it is well known in other places : —

> "If that to ring you would come here,
> You must ring well with hand and ear.
> But if you ring in spur or hat,
> Fourpence always is due for that.
> But if a bell you overthrow,
> Sixpence is due before you go.
> But if you either swear or curse,
> Twelvepence is due; pull out your purse.
> Our laws are old, they are not new;
> Therefore the Clerk must have his due.
> If to our laws you do consent,
> Then take a Bell; we are content."

This church boasts a fresco, supposed to represent Dinoth, to whom reference will be made presently. It has also a good internal roof, now coming well into view during the process of restoration.

Standing here on Bangor Bridge, the eager student of church-history finds his mind strangely drawn over a wide range of theological and ecclesiastical topics. The annals of the Early British Church are but dimly recorded; but so far as they can be ascertained, or even reasonably guessed at, they possess extraordinary interest; and in no place is this interest so definitely concentrated as in Bangor Monachorum. Pelagius, who has been described as the first Briton who ever distinguished himself in literature or theology, is connected by a probable tradition with this spot; and the name of Pelagius carries our thoughts at once to Italy and Palestine and North Africa, and indeed over the whole area of Christianity of the fifth century. This is not the occasion for estimating the subtle and evasive dialectics of this eminent man. Fuller says shrewdly, that "every man is born a Pelagian;" and at all events the opposing views of Augustine have been, on the whole, accepted by Christendom since. Leaving aside all speculation, and attending to our proper subject, we are startled by finding that the history of Pelagianism brings us back to the Dee again. The opinions expressed by this name prevailed so much in Britain, and were held to be so mischievous that Germanus, Bishop of Auxerre, was sent to combat them. The Council at St. Alban's, in which this question was debated, forms the subject of one of the " Stories of the Early British Church," by the reverend author of the " Rectory of Valehead " (himself a Welshman, whose early home was not very far from the Dee); as does also a military victory, won, under singular circumstances,

Bangor Bridge.

by the Britons over the Picts and Saxons in the neighbourhood of this stream, through the help of Germanus. The Britons, in their terror, invited him to the border of Wales near Chester. It happened that a large number of Christian converts had just been baptized in the Alyn, which will hereafter be noted as one of the tributaries of the Dee. These men Germanus placed

in ambush, with instructions at a given signal to shout "Hallelujah!" with all their might. This shout, "much multiplied by
the advantage of the echo," surprised the Pagans; and, "besides the concavity of the valleys improving the sound, such a
hollowness was cast into their hearts, that their apprehensions
added to their ears," and they fled in confusion, and many of
them were drowned; and "that which had been the Christians'
font became the Pagans' grave." What degree of literal truth
there is in this story we cannot tell; but it is mentioned by
Gregory the Great, not very long afterwards, in his meditations
on the Book of Job; and the name Maes-German, or "the Field
of Germanus," preserves still the tradition of the "Hallelujah
victory" near the banks of the Alyn.

But it is at Bangor Monachorum itself, and in connection
with another Augustine, that an event more important in the
Early British Church, and more definitely authenticated, took
place. Gregory had now sent his great missionary to convert
the Anglo-Saxons, and those conferences on minor points with
the British Church took place which were marked (perhaps we
may justly say this) by arrogance on one side, and obstinacy
on the other. The two spots most distinctly associated with
these struggles are "Augustine's Oak" on the Severn, and
Bangor on the Dee. That interview had occurred, which produced so much irritation, and the circumstances of which may
be given from an old writer in the odd spelling that always
seems to make a story of this kind more real. The British
Bishops, with Dinoth, Abbot of Bangor, being in perplexity as
to how they should deal with the demands of Augustine, sought
advice from a holy anchorite, who spoke as follows:—"'If this
same Augustine bee a meeke and humble-minded man, it is a
great presumption that he beareth the yoke of Christ and offreth
the same unto you; but if he be stout and proud, he is not of
God, and you may be bold. This, therefore,' quoth he, 'is my

advice: have a care that he and his company be first in the place when you meete: if then, you being the greater number, he rise not to do you reverence, but despise you, despise you also him and his counsell.' Augustine, therefore, first entered the place, with his banner and his crosse, with singing procession, and great pompe; and when the Brittane Bishops came in, never mooved to rise or saluted them at all. This they taking very ill gainsaid him in every thing, exhorting one another not to yeild a iote with him by any means. 'For,' said they, 'if hee will not daine so much as to rise out of his chayre to salute us, how much more, when we have once submitted ourselves to his jurisdiction, will he despise us and set us at nought?'" So the interview ended with open hostility, when, as it seems to us, there ought to have been peace. Then followed Augustine's prophecy that if the British Christians would not submit and join the Roman Christian in converting the Saxons, they would soon feel the force of the Saxon sword. This prophecy was before long terribly fulfilled. The Pagan king of Northumbria, having conquered Chester, invaded Wales—declared that if the monks of Bangor prayed against him, they were his enemies—slew them, to the number, it is said, of twelve hundred—and burnt their monastic buildings along the Dee in a great conflagration.

The moral lesson and the historical importance of this occurrence are alike obvious. It is to be hoped that we need not believe what some authors allege, that Augustine designed the death of these British monks, "so that he cunningly foretold what he himself cruelly intended to fulfil," just as Jezebel, who is called a prophetess, "could certainly foreshadow the death of Naboth, when she had purposely beforehand packed and plotted the same." Certain it is that the heathen Saxons were more willing to listen to the Italian Christians than to the British, and that the great conversion effected under Augustine brought this island within the general range of European history. For every reason this tragedy at Bangor Monachorum deserves the pause which we have made in following the "holy" stream: and the stream at this point may well seem to have been rendered more holy by this occurrence. The sad poetry of the event has struck many minds, and, among others, the mind of Sir Walter Scott, who, in a short ballad, sings of Chester beleaguered by the heathen; of Bangor's holy anthem "floating down the sylvan Dee;" of the peaceful monks struck down and slaughtered; and of the shattered ruins, which "long told the tale."

Such ruins are mentioned by writers in the Middle Ages; but they have now altogether disappeared. Pennant does, indeed, describe and delineate certain tombs and crosses which he found on the spot; and it is interesting to remark that the Art which decorates them resembles very closely the ornamentation of similar monuments at Iona, and along the coast of Argyllshire, and in the Isle of Man. But nothing of this kind now remains at Bangor. We must be content with the history and the poetry which cannot be taken away from us, and with the general aspect of the place.

Somewhat less than half way between Bangor and Holt, the Dee quits entirely the detached eastern portion of Flintshire, and constitutes itself, through a series of extraordinary sinuosities, the boundary between Denbighshire and Cheshire. But in touching the county of Cheshire, we enter upon so new and so important a part of our general subject, that it is best to place it in a fifth chapter, for which Farndon Bridge will give us a definite starting-point. The scenery here is very beautiful, the high banks of the Dee often densely covered with trees that descend to the water's edge.

V.

THE ROMANS ON THE DEE.

APPROACH TO CHESTER—MALPAS—BISHOP HEBER—WREXHAM—THE ALYN—RICHARD WILSON—EATON HALL—THE SALMON OF THE DEE—ROMAN OCCUPATION OF CHESTER —THE TWENTIETH LEGION—ROMAN REMAINS IN CHESTER.

N crossing the bridge from Holt to Farndon (and this bridge, as will be noted hereafter, is, for every reason, worthy of the most careful attention) we pass decisively out of Wales into England.   It is not indeed till we have travelled some little distance below Farndon that the Dee becomes altogether a Cheshire river.   Still, the county of Chester does at this bridge begin to claim the river as her own ; and the Dee never again absolutely re-enters Wales.   It is to this part of its course then that the words of Drayton properly belong, when in the preamble to his Eleventh Song, he says :

> " The Muse, her native earth to see,
> Returns to England over Dee ; "

and when he says more fully, and with no little enthusiasm towards Cheshire :

> " The Muse from Cambria comes, with pinions summ'd and sound ;
> And, having put herself upon the English ground,
> First seizeth in her course the noblest Cestrian shore,
> Of our great English bloods as careful here of yore
> As Cambria of her Brute's now is, or could be then :
> For which our proverb calls her, *Cheshire, chief of men.*"

This high compliment to Cheshire, which he repeats below in speaking of those "mightiest men of bone, in her full bosom bred," will not be deemed altogether undeserved by those who have been present at the annual meeting of the county yeomanry in Chester.

Again, we must remember that in prosecuting our task,

> "And following Dee, which Britons long ygone
> Did call 'divine,' that doth by Chester tend,"

to quote the words of Spenser, we are not simply traversing the county of Chester, but approaching very closely to the city itself— "the fortress upon Dee"—"fair Chester, call'd of old Carlegion." Hence it will be quite natural to combine with the remarks that follow some notices of the Roman occupation of this spot, and of the Legion which made it famous. It is, indeed, no anachronism, and no undue liberty taken with geography, to connect the Romans with this reach of the Dee; for they came this way on that campaign which ended with the reduction of Anglesey and with the occupation of this part of England for four hundred years.

In the last chapter a word was said of the extraordinary sinuosities which mark the path of the river, from the point where it leaves behind the detached part of Flintshire till its arrival at Farndon bridge. During this part of its course, one bank is Welsh and the other English. Denbighshire is on one side, and Cheshire on the other. If we extend our view to the rising grounds, which may justly be called the outer edges of the basin of the Dee, we find Malpas and Wrexham looking at one another, from these English and Welsh sides, with an intervening distance of about ten miles. It will be no deviation from our subject if a few lines are given to both these places.

The name of Malpas, as well as its topography, marks it out as having been in old times a "bad step" in many a border campaign between the English and the Welsh. A curious legend connects this topography with one of the parochial peculiarities of the place. This parish has two medieties, called the Upper and Lower Rectories. It is said that a king, detained here by difficulty of travelling, went into the village tavern, and found there the Curate, who, while making himself very agreeable to the visitor, complained of his own hard lot, in contrast with that of the absentee Rector ; on which the monarch enacted that the endowments of the rectory should be divided : whence came a well-known Cheshire proverb, " Higglety-pigglety: Malpas shot." It would detain us too long if we were to analyse this proverb minutely ; and it would spoil the story if we were to attempt to ascertain the name of the king to whom was due the parochial arrangement which still continues. To the Upper Rectory we must pay a visit, and this for more reasons than one. In this house Bishop Heber was born in 1783. Those were days of much greater parochial dignity than that to which we are accustomed now. Every Sunday morning, Heber's father, who then held this Upper Rectory, used to drive in a carriage and four, from his own door (though the distance was not many yards), through the avenue of fine trees to the Church. The position of the Church and Rectory is very striking ; and from the rising ground behind, a noble view is obtained of the valley of the Dee, the Welsh hills beyond Wrexham forming the background.

It is singular that Bishop Heber forms a connecting link between Malpas and Wrexham, which carries our thoughts at once across the intervening valley, from the one to the other. When he was a young man, missionary sermons were not so frequent as they are now ; and on one occasion when he was staying with Dean Shirley, Vicar of Wrexham, his father-in-law, such a sermon was to be preached, and the want of a suitable hymn was felt. He was asked on the Saturday to write one ; and, seated at a window of the old Vicarage house, he produced, after a short interval, in his clear handwriting, with one single word corrected, that hymn beginning, " From Greenland's icy mountains," with which we are all familiar. It was printed that evening, and sung the following day in Wrexham Church. The writer of these pages on the Dee saw the original manuscript some years ago in Liverpool, and more recently he has seen the printer, still living in Wrexham, who set up the type when a boy.

Wrexham is too remote from the very edge of the river to justify here a long pause, though in itself well deserving of a description at leisure. Besides the old vicarage, it has other buildings of great interest, especially the College House near the churchyard. Nor ought we to omit a reference to the "halls," where its markets have been held from very ancient times. The "Yorkshire Hall" for woollen goods has very recently undergone a complete transformation which the antiquary must regret: but the "Birmingham Hall," with its penthouse running round an open court, and with its little numbered store-rooms, reminds us easily of days long gone by. The Church of St. Giles, however, is the pride of Wrexham. Its singular monumental inscriptions are celebrated. Its tower, finished and enriched with statuary about the year 1500 by the aid of indulgences, is visible all the country round.

Wrexham Church.

We are here on the first plateau above the valley of the Dee; and from this point the traveller by railroad on his way towards

Chester descends by a steep incline, first running parallel with the
Alyn, and then crossing it, where it makes a sudden bend. This
stream must be classed with the Ceiriog, as a tributary of the Dee
demanding special notice.

The Alyn, in that part of its course to which reference has just
been made, is a prettily fringed stream, with a very steep bank on
one side. But we must not forget the beauty of its earlier windings
through the hill country above. Pennant dwells upon this beauty
with a true love of Nature and the indigenous pride of a Welshman.
Speaking of a particular spot near Mold, he says : "I hung long
over the charming vale which opens here. Cambria here lays
aside her majestic air, and condescends to assume a gentler form,
in order to render her less violent in approaching union with her
English neighbour. It were to be wished she had acted with
more moderation, and not outshone it at a rate the most partial
Saxon must allow it to have done." At the distance of some
miles below Mold, the Alyn passes near the old fortress of
Caergwele, and there for about half a mile runs underground. This
fact has been seized upon by Drayton with his usual exactitude of
observation, and in its true relation to the general geography of the
district he is describing. After mentioning some minor tributaries,
he adds :

> " Then Alen makes approach, to Dee most inly dear,
> (Taking Tegiddog in), who, earnest to be there
> For haste, twice underground her crystal head doth run."

Hasting, however, as we must, to rejoin the Dee, we cannot forget
either the sweet scenery of Gresford, amid which the Alyn lingers,
before his tributary course is done, or the eminent landscape-
painter, whose name is peculiarly associated with this affluent of
the Dee.

The date of Richard Wilson is well fixed for us by the story
which is told of him in connection with a dinner, at which Reynolds
and Gainsborough were present. The courtly Sir Joshua had no

liking for the rough honesty and irritable temper of "poor Richard," and in drinking the health of Gainsborough, toasted that artist, with pointed emphasis, as "the best landscape-painter in England," on which Wilson rejoined, "Yes, and the best portrait-painter, too." Wilson was himself one of the founders of the Royal Academy, and became its second librarian. At first he painted portraits, but while he was in Italy, Zuccarelli and Vernet encouraged him to believe in his own genius for landscape; and, as Allan Cunningham says, "he found himself better prepared for this new pursuit than he imagined: he had long been insensibly storing his mind with the beauties of natural scenery; and the picturesque mountains and glens of his native Wales had been to him an academy when he was unconscious of their influence." The story, however, of his life is sad and depressing. The love of landscape was not then what it is now. Moreover it does not, like portrait-painting, make any appeal to vanity. While Wilson lived in London, many of his pictures went wet from the easel to the pawnbroker's, and he is said to have painted one for part of a Stilton cheese and a pot of porter. He was conscious, however, of his own powers. He said once to Sir William Beechey, "You will live to see great prices given for my pictures:" and this estimate has been justified. When he was now an old man, the legacy of a small estate on the Alyn, and the opening of a vein of lead, placed him in affluence. But it was too late. On one of his favourite walks, near Colomendy, he sank exhausted: his sagacious dog brought servants to his aid; but he never recovered. He is buried at Mold. His memory is preserved at Colomendy by the sign of the "Three Loggerheads," two only being exhibited in the picture by Wilson, the third being the visitor who looks at them. There is a better memorial still in his view of the valley of the Alyn, as seen from the Bwlch, near Mold. To this must be added, on the present occasion, a picture of the Dee, taken from a well-known point of view not very far below the point where the tributary joins the main river.

In following the Alyn to its junction with the Dee, we have already been brought to a point some considerable distance below Farndon and Holt; but Farndon Bridge, as well as Holt Church, which has been well restored by Mr. J. Douglas under difficult circumstances, will recall us hereafter to this part of the river. We must now hasten to the river-approaches of Chester itself; and first a pause is imperative at Eaton Hall.

In the chapter which is to be written hereafter on the Castles and Halls of the Dee, the superb buildings which have recently been completed at Eaton, with its gardens and adjacent park, will justly have the most prominent place. At present only a few slight remarks are possible concerning the recent architectural changes which have been made on this spot, and concerning its early historical associations.

Even since the beginning of this century the brick mansion built by Sir John Vanbrugh was standing here, in the midst of gardens laid out according to the taste that reigned in the time of William III. This house was entirely demolished, to make way for a Gothic structure, which, though extremely costly and elaborate, was disappointing. That was the time when the feeling for Gothic architecture was reviving in this country, but its principles were not yet understood. And now a new pile of buildings, of great extent and grandeur, has taken the place of the pseudo-Gothic mansion.

The site deserves to be distinguished by architectural splendour; for it is the early home of a feudal family very closely connected with the coming of William I., and, indeed, through Hugh Lupus, personally connected with the Conqueror himself. A manuscript in the Library at Eaton is a curious record of the eminence of the Grosvenors, at the time when heraldic differences were held to be of very serious importance. This is the account of the great trial, in the reign of Richard II., between Sir Robert le Grosvenor and Sir Richard le Scrope, as to the right of bearing certain arms; and there is an obvious fitness in referring to this manuscript in connection with the Dee; for among the witnesses whose signatures are given, along with John of Gaunt and Geoffrey Chaucer, is Owen Glendower.

Salmon Fishing opposite Chester Castle.

One privilege attached to this family, and prominently mentioned in records of about this same date, was "the Serjeantry of the

F

Dee," in reference to the salmon for which this river is famous. The fishery at this point was formerly of great importance. The Rector of Eccleston, a charming village close to Eaton, claimed every twentieth salmon as part of his tithe. More will be said on this subject hereafter, when we have passed "The King's Pool," below Chester Bridge, and find ourselves among the nets which are busily used where the river approaches the sea. But the active and subtle life of the salmon connects the salt water and the fresh: and the subject could not have been altogether unnoticed in this part of the " wizard stream."

In floating down from Eccleston to Chester we are conscious of having reached a totally new passage in the progress of the Dee. The water is no longer as at Llangollen, where (to quote a Welsh writer), "emblematic of its country, it runs with great passion through the valley," but its surface is broad and calm, and overhung with trees, reminding us of some of the tranquil river-scenery of the Thames. On a warm summer evening this reach of the Dee is diversified with pleasure-boats: in a severe winter it is covered with skaters: in the solitary and dewy freshness of a spring morning, it is perhaps more delightful than at any other time. When we pass beyond the trees and reach the level ground on the left, round which the deep water of the river sweeps in a broad curve, we have Chester before us: and here we pause, with a very definite passage of history in our thoughts.

The arrival of the Romans in this place impressed upon it a military distinction, which was well sustained afterwards, in the times of William I., Edward I., and Charles I. The conquest, too, of Britain by the Romans, was the first event which brought our island within the range of general European history. It was remarked in the preceding chapter that a similar result was due to the mission of St. Augustine: but it must not be forgotten that there was an earlier period also when the island was part of the great European system, the interval between the two periods being defined by the breaking up of the Roman Empire, when Britain was occupied by the heathen Saxons. It is the earlier Italian invasion and absorption which is now before our attention.

Few things are more curious than the inveterate surviving of the popular fallacy that Julius Cæsar conquered Britain half a century before the Christian era. Half a century, however, after that era was the date of a very real change in the history of this island and the history of the Dee. The invasion under the Emperor Claudius was decisive, and its results proceeded uninterruptedly. There is a high satisfaction in being able to associate the great generalship and noble character of Agricola, quite definitely, with Chester. He came here first in the year 60 A.D., as an officer in the army of Suetonius Paulinus, and subsequently, in the year 77 A.D., he came again as military governor of the newly-conquered province. He remained here seven years, and in his first campaign he reduced North Wales and Anglesey. This, then, is the time to which we must assign the establishment of the Roman troops in a fixed camp on the "Deva." Nor must we forget what Agricola did in teaching the arts of civilised life, and in promoting the education of the sons of British chiefs. Of all these things the memory is imperishably recorded in the name of Chester. We have compound reminiscences of Roman stationary camps in the north-west of England, as at Manchester and Ribchester; but the fortress on the Dee is "Castra," pure and simple.

We have, however, something more definite still to be said in connection with the Roman history of Chester. A famous body of troops, with a distinctive name, is associated with the place. Just as each English regiment has its own annals, which are well remembered from victory to victory, so was it with each imperial legion of Rome. Just as our Twenty-second Regiment has in Chester Cathedral a proud relic in the old flags which were at the taking of Quebec, so does the city still preserve visible and durable memorials of the Twentieth Legion. We must, however, beware of two mistakes into which the parallel might lead us. A Roman legion was much larger than an English regiment; and it was commonly quartered longer in the province to which it was attached than is usual with our troops on any of their foreign stations. A Roman legion consisted of about six thousand foot-soldiers, with a considerable body of cavalry attached : and with these troops were commonly associated an equal number of auxiliaries recruited from the province itself. As to the period of time through which we can trace the existence of this legion, it first comes before our notice near Cologne on the Rhine, soon after the death of Augustus : there seems no doubt that it came over to Britain in the reign of Claudius, under Suetonius Paulinus; and we know that it was engaged in the celebrated action against Boadicea ; nor did it ever leave the island afterwards, till in the fifth century the legions were all recalled from the frontiers of the Empire in consequence of the irruption of the Barbarians. Moreover, from the manner in which Tacitus mentions the Twentieth Legion, it seems evident that it was among the *élite* of the Roman army, and that its steadiness and vigour marked it out for posts of honour. Its title was " Valens Victrix," expressing both its strength and its success. Thus the fact which we have to deal with is the continued presence in this spot, for about four hundred years, of fully ten thousand men, with detachments at various points in the neighbourhood. Such detachments we can trace at two of the spots mentioned in this very chapter, at Holt on the Dee, and at Caergwele on the Alyn. The results in this part of England must evidently have been very marked; and when we consider that Christianity must have been strongly established here, under the legionary soldiers who came about the time when St. Peter and St. Paul were martyred, we feel that some of those results were undoubtedly beneficent. It was a bad day for Chester when the Roman troops marched finally to Italy, and left the Britons on the Dee to their own unassisted resources.

The visible memorials of the Roman period of the history of Chester, though not very copious, are still very distinct, and tell their story clearly. Some have been destroyed within the last hundred years, especially certain arches, which formerly (to compare small things with great) marked one of the old Roman entrances to the city, as the "Porta Nigra" does at Trèves. Within the last ten years, during the removal of an old hotel in Bridge Street,

Roman Altars at Chester.   *Stamp of Tile in Chester, with impression of a Roman Soldier's Foot.*

the ground floor of Roman houses came to view, with fragments of tessellated pavement and other features familiar to us at Pompeii; and one of the hypocausts, or arrangements for warming, can still be seen very complete. There are also coins, and altars, and tombs, all bearing the clear marks of the same period of history. Above all, we must mention the earthenware, the very art of making which was probably introduced into this island by the Romans. We have in Chester their roofing-tiles, their flue-tiles, and their paving-tiles. One of these is of peculiar interest. Across the clearly-impressed mark of the Twentieth Legion, and at right

angles with the inscription, are the indentations of the nails of a
Roman soldier's "caliga," or boot, which must evidently have stood
upon the tile, while it was yet wet. The start of pleasure with
which we see these traces of a definite moment in the past is like

Remains of Roman Wall, Chester.

that which we feel when, at Stourton Quarry, in this county, we
track the footprints of the Labyrinthodon, as first left on the rock
when it was moist sand upon the shore.

And yet, perhaps, the most impressive of all the Roman memorials in Chester are those which could not be collected into a museum, namely, the walls and streets of the city. As regards the walls, the enclosure of modern Chester follows, with the exception of the southern extremity, the line marked out by the Romans : and at one point on the north, where the canal (itself partly following the line of an old Roman excavation) is overshadowed by a fine ash-tree, there are clear courses of imperial masonry, capped by a classical cornice, which, even half-hid here among the weeds, reminds the traveller of what he has seen in Rome. The four main streets of the city, intersecting one another exactly at right angles, along which the market-people come to Chester on Saturdays, are the very lines by which those terrible troops of old communicated with the province on every side of the compass. There is hardly a more striking footprint of history than that which meets us in Antonine's "Itinerary," or Road-book of the Empire, when we see, in the account of a system of roads including York, London, Manchester, and Lincoln, these letters, in large and strong Roman writing—DEVA LEG. XX. VICTRIX.

VI.

THE TWO CATHEDRALS OF CHESTER.

CONCLUSION OF THE SAXON PERIOD—EDGAR ROWED BY VASSAL PRINCES ON THE DEE—
LEGEND OF HAROLD—MARCH OF WILLIAM THE CONQUEROR ON CHESTER—HUGH
LUPUS—THE OLD LINE OF BISHOPS OF CHESTER—ST. JOHN'S MINSTER—EARLY
CHURCH OF ST. PETER AND ST. PAUL—ST. WERBURGH—HER SHRINE IN THE
MIDDLE AGES—BENEDICTINES—ST. ANSELM—RESTORATION OF CHESTER CATHEDRAL
—MENDICANT FRIARS IN CHESTER—PARISH CHURCHES.

VERYWHERE in England the shock of the Norman
Conquest has left an indelible mark: and Chester is
very far indeed from being an exception to this general
rule. On the contrary, the change which is associated
with the name of William I. is forcibly recorded, both on its
military and on its ecclesiastical side, in the City of the Dee. The
ecclesiastical side has been specially chosen for the main subject
and for the illustrations of the following remarks: because Chester
is not only a cathedral city, but a city which possesses two cathedrals; and in close connection with these two buildings it is
singularly rich in reminiscences, both of the closing years of the
Saxon period and the early years of the Norman.

With this thought in the mind, we might go back to the reign
of Edgar the Peaceful: and, indeed, he must by no means be
omitted. For the story of his being rowed by vassal princes over
that quiet reach of the Dee which lies close under the old Cathedral

of St. John's, is not merely a legend expressing poetically the high importance of Edgar's reign, but is judged by careful historians to be an authentic fact. The number of these vassal-kings is not quite certain. It rises, in fact, in the narratives of successive chroniclers from six to eight. But the story shall be given in the old rhymes of a Chester monk :—

> " Kynge Edgar approched the Cite of Legions,
> Nowe called Chestre, specified afore,
> Where viii kynges mette of divers nacions,
> Redy to gyve Edgar reverence and honour,
> Legiance and fidelite, depely sworne ful sore
> At the same cite : after to be obedient
> Prompt at his callying to come to his parliament.

> " From the Castell he went to the water of Dee
> By a prive posturne through walles of the towne.
> The kyng toke his barge with mycle rialte,
> Rowying upwarde to the Churche of Saynt John ;
> The forsayd viii kynges with him went alone.
> Kyng Edgar keyt the storne, as most principall ;
> Eche kyng had an ore to labour withall."

There will be occasion to refer again to Bradshawe, the monk of St. Werburgh's Abbey, from whose panegyric of that saint these lines are taken ; nor is he the only member of that religious house who supplies materials for the subject now in hand.

Higden, another monk of the same Abbey, who preceded Bradshawe in point of time, is one of the chroniclers who relate a curious legend which connects Harold with the immediate neighbourhood of the same Church of St. John, and with the same tranquil part of the water of the Dee. It is no wonder if the English found it difficult to believe that their national hero was really killed at Hastings. He survived in popular traditions, which took various forms. One tradition (and it is quite natural that Higden willingly adopted it) brought him to Chester, and made him live the life of an anchorite in a solitary Chapel, close to St. John's Minster on the Dee. It is even said that he survived till the end of the reign of King Henry II., a story which, if true, would have extended his stay on earth to nearly a hundred and seventy years. It is needless to add that the little ivy-clad chapel near St. John's, on a red rock by the river-side, shows by its architecture that it was built at a period very much later. Still there is pleasure in looking at it with these thoughts in the mind: and this, at least, appears to be certain, that Harold's widow, after that disastrous battle on the coast of Sussex, did retire to the " City of the Legions " in the north-west.

As the waters of the river Dee are rich in recollections of the close of the Saxon period and the beginning of the Norman, so also are the city-walls of Chester, round which the river sweeps in bold broad curves on its way to the sea. And now we must turn to the march of the Conqueror himself upon this city. What has just been said may remind us how deeply moved the heart and imagination of the Saxon people were by all that related to the battle of Hastings: while it also seems to connect King William by a personal link with Chester.

The enclosure of the walls at this time was identical with their old circuit under the Romans, except that a Saxon Princess, Elfreda, the "great Lady of the Mercians," had brought within the line of fortification the high ground on the south, immediately above the river, where the Norman keep afterwards stood. The visit of King William to this place was no light part of his conquest, though it was the last part, and that which made the whole decisive. When all the rest of the country was subdued by him, Chester still held out. It was " the one great city which had not bowed to his might, the one still abiding home of English freedom : " and eager was the desire that it should bravely resist ; so that from all the country around men gave their help in defending its walls.

It was essential that this fortress on the Dee should be reduced : and this was done in 1069. The march of William from York, in the very beginning of that year, was perhaps the most memorable part of his last wonderful campaign. The country through which he brought his army was rugged and wild, and the weather inclement and miserable. What all this means for invading troops on such a march can be imagined even by the modern luxurious traveller, who happens to find himself at the opening of the Penistone tunnel in a snowstorm. The hills, however, between Yorkshire and Lancashire, and the tempestuous season, were not the worst part of the invader's difficulty. A mutinous spirit broke out among the soldiers, and it was necessary to follow Cæsar's example, to tell the loyal to advance and bid the disaffected depart. The iron will of the Conqueror triumphed over all hindrances. The fall of Chester became the last event of his subjugation of this island ; and William established Hugh Lupus, a kinsman of his own, as the great feudal lord on the Dee.

Turning now from the military to the ecclesiastical side of this history, we find in St. John's Church a permanent and very grand memorial of the Early Norman period. In Saxon times Chester was included, with all the extensive tract of Mercia, in the Diocese which acknowledged allegiance to the great see of St. Chad : but with the early Norman kings came a change that made Chester a definite centre of episcopal jurisdiction. This change was part of the course of general policy which led to the removal of sees from comparatively insignificant places to towns of recognised importance. In fact a Council was held in London for fixing certain regulations of this kind. It has been remarked that any one examining the arrangements of the old Dioceses in France would find in them a reproduction of Roman Gaul. Such is not the case, however, with the early ecclesiastical geography of this island. St. David's and Lindisfarne may be named as seats of bishoprics very remote from the concourse of men. Thus obvious reasons existed for removing the see of Sherborne to Old Salisbury, and for fixing at Chester the bishop of the midlands and north-west rather than at Lichfield or Coventry. From the eleventh century to the thirteenth the title of Bishop of Chester appears several times in ancient documents as

Ruins of St. John's, from the Grosvenor Park.

synonymous with that of Bishop of Lichfield or Bishop of Coventry.

Thus we are told that Buildwas Abbey in Shropshire was founded for Savigniacs by the ruler of the Diocese, who is called Bishop of Chester. This ecclesiastical synonym, indeed, gradually passed out

Triforium and Clerestory of St. John's.

of existence: and the episcopal title fell back upon Lichfield and Coventry, where it remained during the later Middle Ages.

Chester, however, still retains on the very edge of its historic river, a striking monument of its early diocesan dignity. The gigantic round Norman piers of the nave stand just as they stood in the days of William Rufus; and the fine triforium above belongs to a period not much later; and though large portions of this structure have been destroyed, and though its partial restoration in modern times is unworthy of its ancient grandeur, yet in two respects this church cannot fail to make a great impression on all

St. John's Church, from the River.

who see it. The ruins at the East-end, recently extricated from heaps of rubbish and the growth of trees, are now a recognised ornament of Chester, near the new park which is laid out on a table-land above the banks of the Dee; while the lofty tower, erect though mouldering, and still showing in parts some faint traces of its old enrichment, is conspicuous in every view of Chester, and rivals in its elevation the tower of the present Cathedral, which stands on the highest ground in the city. To this present Cathedral we must now give our attention.

And again the early sources of what we have to tell of this other church are to be found in Saxon times—in times, indeed, more remote even than the Saxon; for there is good reason to believe that during the Roman occupation of Chester, a church, dedicated to St. Peter and St. Paul, stood upon this spot; and most interesting it is thus to connect this ground with the early Christianity of the Apostle of the Gentiles, so large a part of whose life was spent among Roman soldiers, and whose name must almost certainly have been known to some who fought on the Welsh frontier, and were quartered at Chester, under the successors of Agricola. But in the Saxon ages we enter upon passages of clearer Christian history, and two names come out before us here specially and conspicuously side by side, St. Werburgh and St. Oswald.

Great as may be the amount of legend which has grown up round St. Werburgh's name, it would be quite a mistake to suppose that her story is purely legendary; while her fame in the Middle Ages was so considerable, and her memory is still so distinctly impressed upon the City and Cathedral of Chester, that, if these papers were longer, her life would require from us more than a passing notice. As to her history, let it suffice to say, in words used by Sir G. Gilbert Scott in one of his lectures, that she was a link in "the unbroken chain of saintly princesses which extends from Bertha, the grand-daughter of St. Clotilda, whom we received from France, and whose gentle encouragement introduced Christianity among our race, to St. Margaret, whom we gave to Scotland, and who restored the true royal blood of England to our later kings." She was the daughter of the third of three abbesses of Ely who had been Saxon queens—a fact which is "still symbolized by the three crowns in the arms of that see." In turn she, too, became abbess of Ely: she founded a religious house at Trentham, and there she died; and thence, during the great Danish invasion, her remains were brought to Chester, when this church was re-dedicated by Elfreda, the daughter of King Alfred, in the joint-names of St. Werburgh and St. Oswald. Why these two names are so closely associated here on the banks of the Dee is an intricate question of history, and, indeed, as we shall see presently, of architecture too. But, to proceed with the story of St. Werburgh, her shrine became in the Middle Ages a noted place of pilgrimage, and doubtless a source of great profit. The estimate in which she was then held can be gathered

Chester Cathedral from the North-East, and Part of City Wall.

from the lines written by Bradshawe on the spot, of which the
following may be quoted as a specimen:

> "O rutilant gemme, clerer than the cristall;
> O redolent rose, repleit with suavite,
> Whiche, for the love of thy spouse eternall,
> Refused hast all vague pleasures transetore,
> Honour, riches, and secular dignite,
> Nowe regnyng in hevyn as a quene doutles—
> Praye for thy servaunt to the Lorde of mercy,
> Mekely I beseke thee, swete patronesse.

> "O pereles princes, lady imperiall,
> O gemme of holynes and noble president,
> Comfort to all creatures in paynes thrall—
> Relevyng all secke, feble, and impotent;
> A myrrour of mekenes to every pacient,
> Whose myracles magnifien thy great goodnes—
> Defend thy servaunt from grevous turment
> By thy supplicacion, swete patronesse."

It is a fact of considerable interest that less than four years ago,
during the process of restoring Chester Cathedral, among the
materials with which a wall had been built across the western
extremity of the north aisle of the Nave, new fragments of the
shrine of St. Werburgh were discovered; and it is curious that
this happened about the time when portions of the shrine of
St. Alban, at the great abbey which bears his name, were brought
to light.

But in speaking of the shrine of St. Werburgh, and in quoting
the lines which relate to her, we are anticipating. Neither this
structure of stone nor this poetry belongs to the church which
was erected here before the Conquest, but to one which dates
from the reign of the Conqueror's son. Thus we are brought
down once more to our great historic point. Hugh Lupus, who
has been mentioned as the feudal lord planted among the Saxon
vassals in these parts, came late in life under the influence of
religious thoughts, which at an earlier period seem to have had

G

little power over him; and, according to the feeling of those
times under such circumstances he determined to found an abbey,
in which, in fact, he himself became a monk before his death.   He
sent for Benedictine monks from the great abbey of Bec, in
Normandy, over which Lanfranc, the first Norman Archbishop

Cathedral : Cloisters and King's School.

of Canterbury, had presided.   At the head of these monks came
Anselm, who himself was made Archbishop on his return from
this visit to Chester.   William Rufus had wrongfully kept the
see vacant four years: and, being then confined to his bed in
what was deemed to be fatal illness, and knowing that public

opinion pronounced for Anselm, he sent for that great man to

Cathedral Tower, from Newgate.

his sick chamber, and forced him to become Archbishop. The

story has recently been told with animation by two of our English Deans, in the well-known " Lives of the Archbishops of Canterbury," by the Dean of Chichester, and in a charming monograph on "St. Anselm," by the Dean of St. Paul's.

Thus the present Cathedral Church of Chester, once the Abbey Church of St. Werburgh, has a distinguished lineage, both secular and ecclesiastical ; its joint founders having been a kinsman of William the Conqueror, on the one hand, and, on the other, one of the greatest theologians and one of the most saintly men of the Middle Ages. Architecture, too, remains, in the North Transept of the church, and along the north wall of its Nave, belonging to the precise time when Anselm and Hugh Lupus met here in the reign of the Red King. From this beginning the church grew, in the usual manner, through various alterations and with additions in successive styles. Two very remarkable features may be mentioned, which have recently been brought prominently under public notice in the course of the complete restoration of the whole fabric which is now in progress. The first is the extraordinary conical roof at the end of the south aisle of the Choir, which has now reappeared in the form in which Edward I. saw it, when that monarch liberally aided the Abbot of that day, Simon of Whitchurch in his great architectural works. No such feature is to be seen in any other church in England : but examples are to be found in Normandy : and we have probably in this part of the building an indication of continued and active communication between the Abbey of St. Werburgh in Chester and the Abbey of Bec. The other singular characteristic of this church is the immense size of the South Transept, which is now undergoing repair : and here we encounter the architectural puzzle, which was named above in connection with St. Oswald. This South Transept has been the place of worship for St. Oswald's parish from the time when Henry VIII. made this church a Cathedral Church ; and so it was during the latter part of the period in which it was an Abbey Church. Of the circumstances under which the parishioners obtained their victory over the monks history is provokingly silent. It is to be hoped that amicable feelings will always henceforward subsist, whence once there was contention, between the interests represented by the names of St. Werburgh and St. Oswald.

This is the church which Henry VIII. connected with a new episcopal line at the Dissolution of the Monasteries. We must not, however, travel beyond the limits of the Middle Ages. The Bishops of Chester of the new series belong to a subsequent chapter. Still it is to be remembered that, great as this Abbey was, and great as was St. John's Church, they by no means complete the whole ecclesiastical picture of Chester in the Middle Ages. A few words may be said here in conclusion concerning the Friaries and the Parish Churches of this city of the Dee.

Those who have examined the bills of fare in French *restaurants* may sometimes have had their curiosity excited by observing a dish described in them as "Les quatre Mendiants:" and they have probably been both amused and disappointed to find this means simply a few figs, a few almonds, a few raisins, and

Cathedral : Piscina in North Aisle of Choir.

a few dried plums, so arranged as to represent the four colours of the four Mendicant Orders. These orders were the Dominicans, Franciscans, Carmelites, and Augustinians. They obtained immense powers from the Pope, and rapidly spread over all Europe, to the great discomfort of the parochial clergy. The cities of England presently exhibited in their architecture the visible results of this ecclesiastical change. This was notably the case in Bristol, where Friars of all the four orders have left their mark to this day : and there is little doubt that all these bodies were represented in Chester too, so as to effect the physiognomy of the city from the thirteenth century onward. The streets named Whitefriars and Greyfriars tell their story very plainly concerning Carmelites and Franciscans ; and an extract from an old antiquarian may be given, to show what picturesque effects we have lost by the destruction of their buildings :—"In 1597," says Webb, "the white-freeres steeple, curiously wrought, was taken downe, and a faire house built there by Sir Thomas Egerton, knight, lord keeper: a great pitie that the steeple was put away, being a great ornament to the citie. This curious spire steeple

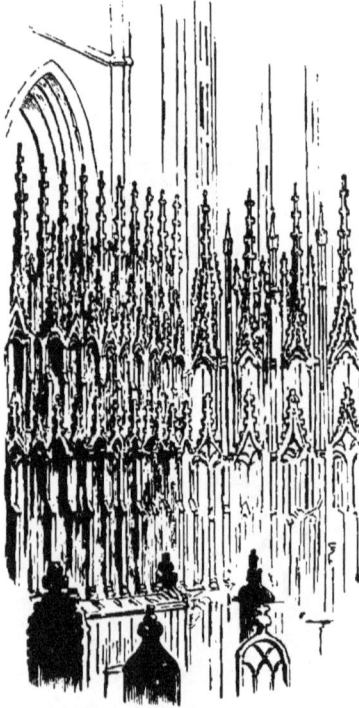

Cathedral : Woodwork in Choir.

might still have stood for grace to the citie, had not private benefit, the devourer of antiquitie, pulled it down with the church, and erected a house for more commodity, which since hath been of little use. So that the citie lost so goodly an ornament, that tymes hereafter may more talk of it, being the only sea-mark for direction over the bar of Chester." The site of this spire was on the west side of Bridge Street : and the mention of this part of the city leads naturally to a remark concerning its Parish Churches as they appeared in the Middle Ages.

St. Peter's, at one extremity of the street, placed just where the four Roman ways intersect each other at right angles, and in its name (though defrauded of the companionship of St. Paul) containing a remembrance of the earliest of all Chester churches, still exhibits architecture which is anterior to the Reformation. The same is true of St. Mary's, on the hill where the old Norman Castle stood, beyond the lower end of Bridge Street, but not true

Cathedral : Pulpit in King's School.

(except to a trivial extent) of any other parish church in Chester. There was a time when Bridge Street must have been singularly curious and pleasing in the light and shade, in the projections and corners, of its church-architecture : for old St. Bridget's stood there on its western side, close under the Carmelite Spire, and opposite

St. Michael's and St. Olave's, with one of which churches it was united by an arch over the street. This state of things has long been obliterated : and St. John's Church and St. Werburgh's Church stand out, pre-eminent and unrivalled, asserting for Chester the honour, which it shares with only one or two other cities in the world, of possessing two Cathedrals.

In May, 1884, a discovery of great interest was made at White-friars. In excavating for a new house the remains of a Roman public building were found at a depth of seven or eight feet below the surface of the street. There were massive columns, and bases, and tesselæ; and there were also tiles of the XX. Legion. The sand-stone of which these remains are composed is much redder and brighter than any we now are acquainted with in these parts.

Above these, and about half-way between them and the surface, were found remains of nine centuries later date. These consisted of a beautifully-tiled floor, and some jambs apparently of the fifteenth century ; they belonged to the monastery of the Whitefriars, or Carmelites, that has been alluded to. They were at once preserved with care by the owner of the building, and added to the antiquities of Chester.

The church of St. Peter is now believed to stand on the site of the old Prætorium. It stands just at the intersection of the cross streets, and in all probability it covers some very interesting Roman remains of all descriptions,

VII.

CHESTER IN THE CIVIL WARS.

ASPECT OF CHESTER DURING THE CIVIL WARS—THE WALLS AND GATES—THE STREETS—
THE "ROWS"—VISIT OF JAMES I.—FIRST VISIT OF CHARLES I.—SIEGE OF THE CITY
—SECOND VISIT OF THE KING—SURRENDER OF THE CITY—THE CITY SWORD AND
MACE.

N a series of twelve chapters on the river Dee, two are not
a disproportionate share to assign to the City of Chester;
and if distinct periods of English history are to be carefully chosen for those two papers, they clearly ought to
be the early part of the Feudal age and the time of the Wars of the
Commonwealth. The former subject having been disposed of, though
far too slightly, in the last chapter, we turn now to similar treatment
of the latter. In regard to this, as in regard to the other, Chester
went through a very exciting and stirring experience, and has
retained many visible memorials.

In this case, as in the former, the interest of the matter with
which we have to deal is partly military and partly ecclesiastical.
In the present paper, however, we will look rather at the municipal
side of our subject; and our best course, in the first place, will be
to take a glance at the aspect of the city at the time when King
Charles I. quarrelled decisively with his Parliament.

The general enclosure of the Walls was just what it had been in
the time of William the Conqueror, and, indeed, just what it is now;

and the citizens in the early part of the sixteenth century walked, as
we walk, on summer evenings, and looked at the boats on the still
water of the river, above the place where it breaks over the broad
"causeway" and takes its course along a lower level towards the
sea. The houses were more restricted within this enclosure than at
present; but still there were considerable suburbs on opposite sides

Water Tower, with Roman Hypocaust.

of the river, at Boughton and at Handbridge, as we shall have
occasion to see presently, when we come to attend to the circumstances of the siege of Chester. The masonry of the walls,
and especially the towers, had been chiefly constructed in the
Edwardian period. Connected with the Gates of the city, at the
time of which we are now thinking, were structures of varied and

expressive forms, the utter demolition of which is deeply to be regretted. As the Dee is our subject, it is worth our while to refer to the two gates by which it was approached. That which opened at the lower end of Bridge Street upon the mediæval bridge, which fortunately still remains, was distinguished by a very tall tower. The descent of Watergate Street, at right angles to Bridge Street, led to the Dee at another point of its broad, sweeping course. Of the actual form of the gate there is less to be recorded ; but a little beyond this spot the Water Tower (sometimes called the New Tower), remains at the northwestern angle of the city, so as to show us very vividly what the general aspect was of this part of the walls in the time of Charles I. Probably the Dee wandered very freely, at high water, close under the walls of this tower, which still exhibits iron staples, showing that ships were anciently moored at the place. It would be a mistake,

Old House and Row in Northgate Street.

however, to suppose that this could have been the case during the Civil Wars. Fuller, who wrote at the time of the Restoration, says, on taking his leave of "this ancient and honourable

city," that the worst he can wish it is this, that the distance between
Dee and the New Tower may be made up, all obstructions being
removed which cause or occasion the same—"that the rings on
the New Tower (now only for sight) may be restored to the service
for which they were first intended, to fasten vessels thereunto—that
vessels on that river (lately degenerated from ships into barks) may
grow up again to their former strength and stature."

Turning now from the outside of the walls to the inside, we must
remember that the four Roman Streets, intersecting one another at
right angles, have always been the features which determined the
whole interior character of the city. Only we must add to this fact
that at the intersection was the " High Cross " itself—a structure of
stone, which was demolished when Cromwell became victorious—and
that closely attached to St. Peter's Church was a municipal building
called the Pentice, with gables in its roof and rich woodwork in its
front. Several residences of this period remain, from which we can
infer the general character of the whole; and especially we must
notice certain houses in Northgate and Foregate Streets, outside the
walls—standing, as it were, over the footway, each with two legs or
more planted at the edge of the street—if we wish to take into
account all the elements supplied by Chester for helping our recollection of the Civil Wars. But, above all, we must attend to the
"Rows" which were then, as now, quite unique. No archæological
and pictorial delineation of the Dee would be complete without some
notice of these singular arrangements in the streets of its ancient
city.

The Chester "Rows" are not simply covered ways for foot-
passengers, along the sides of the streets and on the same level, such
as are found in many Continental cities; they are covered galleries,
raised several feet above the street, so that there are shops under
the feet of those who walk to and fro, while the front rooms of overhanging houses are above their heads. Thus there is this singular
fact in Chester, which it shares with no other city, that, partly

along the pathway supplied by the Walls, partly by the aid of
these Rows, the foot-passengers can move about on a higher
level than the carriages and the horses. Flights of steps at short
intervals connect the Rows with the Streets. The nearest resem-

Ancient Half-Timbered Houses, Foregate Street.

blance to this arrangement in any foreign city is at Berne, where
in the lower part of the central street—the ground there falling
rapidly towards the place where children and English travellers
feed the bears—the covered footway does become a Row, because

the space beneath it becomes sufficient for vaults and shops. But it is a strange fact that the truest prototype of the Chester Row is to be found in a relic of ancient Classical Rome. Not that any continuous architectural tradition from so ancient a date can be suggested with confidence. And yet these Rows have probably something to do, in their origin, with the early

Bridge Street Row.

Roman times. Stukely, in his "Itinerary," written not much more than half a century after the death of Charles I., says : "The Rows, or piazzas, of Chester are singular through the whole town, giving shelter to the foot people : I fancied it a remain of the Roman portico." And probably no better suggestion to explain the beginning of this street-arrangement has been given than that in Hemingway's

" History " of this city. He remarks that the central place of the Roman garrison on the Dee was where the streets intersect each other, that it was desirable to provide full employment for the soldiers, and that a reduction of the level of the upper part of Watergate and Bridge Streets was evidently convenient. "It is also worthy of remark," he adds, "in considering this question, that these were the only streets which had an immediate communication with the waters of Dee. The river encompassed the lower parts of both ; and either at one or the other it was of course necessary to land warlike stores, forage, and provisions, or other heavy materials." This explanation may or may not be correct ; but this fact is certain, that the Rows were in Chester during the siege, and that under their shelter, in driving rain, or hot sunshine, the citizens were often, at that anxious time, in serious consultation together. Two things more must be added, in order that we may bring back these

Roman Base and Shaft of Column found in Bridge Street, Chester

scenes more correctly : little shops along the outer edges of the footways themselves were more numerous than they are now, and the shops within the shelter of the Rows, on the side furthest from the street, were not glazed, but closed at night with shutters, which in the day were fastened with hooks above the heads of the people.

It is time, however, that we turn from this outward framework of our picture to the historical events which form the picture itself; and it is worth while to glance first at a visit paid by King James I.

to this ancient and singular city in the year 1617, just a quarter of a century before the first visit paid to it by his unhappy son. Attended by bishops, noblemen, and the gentry of the county,

Old Houses in Bridge Street.

he entered by the East gate, where, and along Eastgate Street itself, were posted the "train-bands" of the city, "every company with their ensigns in seemly sort." The mayor and aldermen took their places "on a scaffold, vailed and hung about with green; and there, in most grave manner, attended the coming of his Majesty." The mayor presented the city sword to the king, and received it back, and then bore it on horseback before the king, who rode first to the Minster, where he alighted from his horse. At this point of his progress, "in the West Aisle of the Minster," he heard an oration in Latin, delivered by a scholar of the King's School, after which he went to the Choir and heard an anthem. In those days the King's School was the refectory of the cathedral, and it was well adapted for the transformation; but it has since that time been removed to a new building which occupies the site of the Abbot's palace, and, at the dissolution of monasteries, was converted into the residence of the Bishops of Chester ; and, as it happens, Mr. Blomfield, of London, whose father once filled the see of Chester and occupied this old palace, was the architect of the new building. It is pleasing and picturesque, and when the chemistry of time shall have matched its tints to all the surrounding buildings it will look as if it had formed at one time a part of the old conventual ranges that at one time must have filled Chester with delight.

The troubles of the Civil War, though very tragical for Chester in the end, open in a manner almost ludicrous. We learn from Lord Clarendon that " the city was firm to the King by the virtue of its inhabitants." Thus we are not surprised that when in August, 1642, certain disaffected persons caused a drum to be beaten publicly in the streets, and invited the citizens to enlist themselves on the side of the Parliament, the Mayor, having expostulated with these people, and being contumeliously treated, seized one of them by the collar and delivered him to the constables, then wrested a broadsword from another of the party, cut the drum to pieces, and secured the drummer. This occurrence was speedily followed by the posting of guards, night and day, at the city gates and at the High Cross, by a general assessment of £500, which was the precursor of heavy successive burdens borne afterwards, and by the construction of defensive outworks, which, beginning at a certain alcove, popularly called Pemberton's Parlour, between the North Gate and the Water Tower, and, ranging round by Flookersbrook, came down to St. John's Church—thus showing us how the "wizard stream," which is the true subject of these papers, was viewed as the natural and sufficient defence of the city elsewhere.

The King made Lord Byron Governor of Chester and Colonel-General of the surrounding district, Sir William Brereton being chief of the Parliamentarians, and having his headquarters at Nantwich. Presently came the first visit of Charles himself. He arrived from Stafford along the same line of street as his father before him, and was received with similar formalities. The sword

H

was given and returned, and then borne before him to the Pentice, where he was entertained, his lodging at night being the Bishop's Palace, on the spot where the house of the Abbots had stood, and where Bishop Keene afterwards erected the Episcopal residence, which has recently been converted into the new King's School. Charles I. departed from the city sooner than was expected, crossing the Dee towards Wrexham, in consequence of intelligence which he had received from Prince Rupert of success obtained at Worcester; and now the serious business of the Civil War in Chester began.

The first events of the war caused the garrison and citizens of Chester to be very sanguine in their hopes. Two strong positions on the West and East, Hawarden and Beeston, were gallantly taken, through the co-operation of Loyalist troops recently arrived from Ireland. Sir William Brereton seemed, for the time, to be hemmed in at Nantwich. Gradually, however, and amid various alternations of fortune, he made a serious impression on Boughton, the suburb beyond the East Gate, where, as well as at Handbridge, on the further side of the old Dee Bridge, houses were razed lest they should afford permanent shelter to the assailants. Among the most characteristic and amusing circumstances connected with the siege (if amusement is an allowable feeling in reference to a matter so grave) was the official correspondence which took place between the besiegers and the besieged. Two specimens may be given of letters written on each side. The following is part of one addressed to Lord Byron: —" Although our condition be such that we need not court you, and notwithstanding your scornful rejection of former summons, to clear our innocence before God and men of desiring the effusion of Christian blood, or the ruin of this ancient city, we once more demand the same, with the castle and fort, for the use of the King and Parliament;" in reply to which, Lord Byron and the Mayor begin thus: " Your letter of summons intimating a former letter to the same purpose (which never came to either of our hands or knowledge) we have received, and must thereto return this answer; that we neither apprehend your condition to be so high, nor ours (God be thanked) to be so low, as to be threatened out of this city; and that we have received of his Majesty's express command for the keeping thereof, and therefore cannot, without his Majesty's knowledge, breake so great a trust lay'd upon us." This was in October, 1644. In the following month we find further communications of the same kind. Thus Sir William Brereton writes to Lord Byron, and the Mayor and Aldermen: "When I call to mind those ancient and honourable privileges and immunities which the citizens and freemen of the city of Chester have purchased by their faithful service to this kingdom, I cannot but attempt all fair means on my part that may prevent the loss and destruction of so famous a city and the effusion of blood which must needs ensue, upon your continuance in that way you are in against the Parliament and Kingdom." The retort is addressed to "Sir W. Brereton, Kt. and Bart.," in the Foregate Street. "When we call to mind those ancient and honourable privileges and immunities granted heretofore to the citizens and freemen of the city of Chester, for their loyalty to the Crown, we cannot but wonder at your impertinence in using that as an argument to withdraw us from our allegiance, whereby (if all other respects were forgotten) we are most obliged unto it, even in point of gratitude, as well as conscience. The care you have professed to preserve this city and to avoid the effusion of blood is so much contradicted by your actions, that you must excuse us if we give credit rather to your deeds than your words." The mention of the Foregate in this correspondence shows how close the pressure was at this moment on the city, and causes a great interest to be attached to the older houses on this spot. For another reason, too, the place is made memorable in connection with this history: for the City Sword and City Mace being here at the Mayor's residence, they fell into the possession of the assailants, and were sent up at this time to the Parliament as a trophy.

The second coming of the King to Chester may justly be taken as the turning-point of the siege, and indeed of the war itself; and in these pages it must be noted with the greater care, because in reference to this moment, the City Walls still retain a conspicuous remnant of monumental history. Great delight was caused to the loyal garrison by the visit of their monarch at this critical time. This visit, however, was like the gleam of sunshine that sometimes comes at noon on a cloudy day, which darkens once more and ends in settled rain. We do not read· of any gay reception of King Charles in September, 1645, as when he came two years before. This we know, however, that he was lodged in Lower Bridge Street, just opposite St. Olave's Church.

King Charles' Tower: from the Walls.

Apparently he had entered by that street; for the region outside the East Gate was uncomfortably in the power of the enemy; and we find that while the King was approaching, Sir Marmaduke Langdale, with most of the horse, had been despatched over Holt

Bridge, so as to be on the Cheshire side of the Dee. The action which took place on Rowton Heath was disastrous : and from the leads of the Phœnix Tower, at the north-eastern angle of the walls (the houses in Boughton being in a great measure destroyed, so that the view in that direction was far more free than it could be now), the King saw his troops defeated. It is stated by Randle Holme, a contemporary archæologist who was then in the city, that the King watched this disaster from the roof of the Cathedral also. Nothing is more likely than that from both positions those anxious eyes were directed towards the south-east. The tower, however, on the wall is rightly shown to all tourists in connection with this passage of English history. It is not a little curious that the inscription which is placed upon it is incorrect in its date. The true day was September 27th ; and on the following day the King departed, marching over the Dee Bridge towards Denbigh, and giving orders to Lord Byron, the governor, and the commissioners, " that, if after ten days, they saw no reasonable prospect of relief, they must treat for their own preservation."

The catastrophe soon came. Chester was surrendered on very honourable conditions ; and the cause of Charles I. was lost in the

Mace and Sword of Cor-poration of Chester.

North-West of England, as, in the period in which our attention was last directed, the cause of William I. was won, by the taking of the City on the Dee. One condition of the surrender was, that none of the churches of the city should be defaced. We find, however, that the fonts of the Parish Churches were removed, and that in other

respects the agreement was not kept. At this time the Sword and Mace of the Corporation were restored.

These two last-mentioned municipal insignia are so vividly connected with the history which has just passed rapidly under review, and with other passages of Cestrian history too, that it is not out of place to bring them prominently before the reader's eye. The ponderous Sword of State was given to this city by King Richard II., shortly before his disgrace at Flint Castle, a little lower down the banks of the Dee. Henry VII., in 1506, expressly ordained that the mayor and his successors "shall have this Sword carried before them with the point upwards in the presence of all the nobles and lords of the realm of England;" and such has been the honour always accorded to this Sword, when it has appeared in public in conjunction with the Mace—except, indeed, on two occasions, when certain members of the Cathedral Chapter resisted. In one of these cases, however, the Bishop, in the other, the Mayor, successfully interfered; so that the privilege remains intact. It must be added that the present Mace of the Corporation of Chester is not that which was taken during the siege and restored at its close. The "bauble" now in use was given by Charles, Earl of Derby, "Lord of Man and the Isles," when Mayor of Chester in 1668; and two years later the old historic Mace (first displayed, as it appears, in 1508, at the laying of the foundation-stone of the unfinished south-western tower of the Cathedral) was made over to a goldsmith in exchange for new plate.

VIII.

THE BRIDGES AND FERRIES OVER THE DEE.

SPECIAL INTEREST OF BRIDGES—THEIR CONNECTION WITH HUMAN SOCIETY—LLANGOLLEN
—HISTORICAL ASSOCIATIONS OF ITS BRIDGE—AQUEDUCT AND VIADUCT OVER THE DEE
—TELFORD—ERBISTOCK—BRIDGE BETWEEN HOLT AND FARNDON—ITS CONNECTION
WITH THE CIVIL WAR—CROSSING THE DEE IN A TUB—ALDFORD—FERRY AT ECCLESTON.

ET any one with an imaginative and sympathetic mind
turn his thoughts to the subject of bridges over rivers,
and he will presently find himself diligently occupied and
well rewarded.

In the first place, the presence of a bridge is often determined by
some physical feature in the course of a river, which feature is on its
own account worthy of attention. There may be some bend in the
stream, or some depression of the banks, or some convenient approach
of projecting rocks, with corresponding beauties of flowers and
foliage and deep silent pools. To such a place the children, made
familiar with it through the existence of the bridge, come and gather
garlands, and watch the curious habits of the fish. Such a thought
as this leads us to that which is the main point of the case, the
human interest of these crossing-places over rivers. Bridges cause
friendly neighbourhood where otherwise there would be separation.
Bridges promote mutual acquaintance and the interchange of business. They are associated with all the useful intercourse of civilised
life. We are obliged to add, also, that too often they are associated

with the cruel discord and conflict of human life. Great engineering
skill, again, is often lavished on their construction. This we see more

Llansaintffraid Bridge.

especially when we take into account, as we are bound to do, those
aqueducts and viaducts which are really bridges on the great scale.
Hence it is no wonder that a large amount of history seems to gather

round the structures of this class. What annals, for instance, of the Roman power are bound up with bridges of various kinds, from the old *Pons sublicius* of Lars Porsena, which lives only in ballads, to the *Pont du Gard*, which survives as the most beautiful of all monuments of imperial strength! And in our own country how many struggles of our political growth are imperishably associated with such names as Wakefield Bridge, Stamford Bridge, Bothwell Bridge! What curious mediæval legends, too, are often connected with these places, what anecdotes, what proverbs!

"Follow the river far enough, and you are sure to come to a bridge;" this is a very modern proverb, but it deserves to grow old, for it is a lesson of both patience and hope—a lesson, too, so expressed as to carry our thoughts to pleasant subjects and scenes of beauty. The fact which is the basis of the teaching of the proverb is true of every river of moderate length in a settled and closely peopled country. There cannot be such a stream without its bridges; and to describe such a stream without duly noticing them, would be to incur the blame of a very serious omission.

Boat-house at Queen's Ferry, Lower Dee.

The Dee has its full proportion of Bridges, and in great variety: and with them, on the present occasion, we must include its Fords and its Ferries; for of those more simple and primitive crossing-places much is true that has been said above of the structures of wood, or stone, or iron, that enable us easily to pass from bank to bank. The Bridges which cross at intervals the mountainous part of the Dee, whether the rude and picturesque arches which we find above Bala Lake, or the larger and more elaborate provisions for intercourse between bank and bank which we find in Owen Glendower's valley, must be left unnoticed. Some of them, indeed, find a place in other parts of this series of descriptions. So of the Fords in the earlier part of the "Wizard Stream." There is not yet depth of water sufficient to raise any question of Ferries. We must begin with Llangollen Bridge.

Llangollen Bridge.

The Dee has a very marked character at the place where this bridge crosses its course. Broad flat rocks seem to fill the whole bed of the river when the water is low, and are very visible even when a dark flood —justifying those who would derive the name of the Dee from its blackness—comes rolling down the valley. This feature of the spot attracted the attention of Churchyard, who perhaps deserves that we should quote another stanza from his poem. He has been speaking of Castle Dinas Brân, and he proceeds :—

> " Betweene the towne and abbey built it was:
> The towne is neare the goodly river Dee,
> That underneath a bridge of stone doth passe ;
> And still on rocke the water runnes, you see,
> A wondrous way—a thing full rare and straunge.
> That rocke cannot the course of water chaunge ;
> For in the streame huge stones and rocks remayne
> That backward might the flood of force constrayne."

The bridge itself of Llangollen has a high place in the estimate of all writers on this part of our country: for it is reckoned not only one of the "seven wonders," as has been remarked before, but one of the "three beauties" of Wales. And it is in truth a very good specimen of the mediæval bridge; nor is it without a very interesting connection with history. It was built about A.D. 1350, by John Trevor, afterwards Bishop of St. Asaph. This was the bishop mentioned in an earlier chapter as having urged the House of Lords not to trifle with the incipient rising of the Welsh under Owen Glendower. Previously he had taken an active part in pronouncing the deposition of Richard II., whose meeting with Henry Bolingbroke at Flint was within his diocese; and had been then sent to Spain to present the claims of Henry IV. in a favourable light. Afterwards he withdrew his allegiance from Henry, and joined Glendower. Thus these four irregular pointed arches which cross the Dee at Llangollen

Middle Arches of the Dee Viaduct.

may justly be reckoned to have an historical value, and to be among the things through which "dead times revive."

It is a very sudden transition from this modest work of the Middle Ages to the great triumphs of engineering skill which meet us a few miles lower down the Dee, near its junction with the Ceiriog. Each of these two streams is crossed here by an aqueduct which conveys the water of the Ellesmere Canal, and by a viaduct which forms part of the course of the Great Western Railway; and the grand appearance of the long lines of arches in each instance causes us to rejoice that these works were done before the time of tubular

Aqueduct over the Dee.

bridges, though it is quite possible that the latter are more wonderful results of mechanical contrivance. We are concerned here with the crossing, not of the tributary, but of the Dee itself; and no spot in its whole course is more deserving of a long pause, or more suggestive of thoughts of wonder than when we have before us the arches of Telford's Pont-Cysylltau, strong in their lightness, and

Ferry at Erbistock.

light in their strength. Not that any depreciation is intended of Robertson's great railway-viaduct near the same place. On the contrary, it is most impressive to contemplate the two arches of

this viaduct which span the Dee, and to remember that while a
busy traffic from the principal towns of the kingdom is going over
them, their bases rest in a quiet secluded valley, where the trout are
as undisturbed as ever they were in Glendower's time.   Still the
romance of engineering always seems to be very largely connected
with Telford's name.   It entertains and charms us to think of him,
when he was laid up for a time in Chester in consequence of a blow

Farndon Bridge.

on his leg, as composing his
indifferent verses "On the
Death of Robert Burns," and
to observe the very affectionate
regard which he cherished towards his confidential foreman,
Matthew Davidson.   He seems
quite to forget his own genius
when he says in a letter
written during the progress of
the work: "The vale of Llangollen is very fine, and not the
least interesting object in it, I
can assure you, is Davidson's
famous aqueduct, which is
already reckoned among the
wonders of Wales."

Erbistock has been pre-
viously named as one of the
places near which the Dee is very marked as a county-boundary; and
this is a spot of consummate beauty.   The Dee assumes here, more
than usual, the aspect of a south-country river.   The foliage grows
in great masses to the edge of the water, which lingers through the
trees in a long, deep pool.   The churchyard, near at hand, is shaded
with fine old yews.   It is to be regretted that the church, though
not in itself unpleasing, is hardly in keeping with the character of

the scene. Bangor Bridge, a few miles below, has already been made the occasion of a pause, that some thought might be given to an early passage of Church history connected with the view at this point. We must hasten now to the communication over the river between Holt and Farndon.

This, like the bridge of Llangollen, is mediæval; and, as seen in combination with the low cliff on which Farndon stands, it is a most pleasing object in the landscape. Quite recently it escaped very narrowly from demolition; and we may congratulate all lovers of the ancient and the picturesque that the county authorities on one side of the stream could not agree with the county authorities on the other. Opposite to Farndon are the ruins of Holt Castle, a place which represents a large amount of history, running up into legend. Pennant tells a tragic story of two infant claimants to estates on this part of the Dee being drowned beneath the bridge by their guardians, and of the

Window in Holt Church.

tale becoming current in the country, "under the fable of two young fairies, who had been destroyed in that manner and in that place."

Turning to a more authentic period of history, we must not forget that it was across this bridge that Sir Marmaduke Langdale passed just before the disastrous engagement of Rowton Moor, which Charles I. watched from the towers of Chester. But the mention of his circumstance brings us to a curious mode of ferrying across the river, which signalised this moment of the Civil War. Sir Marmaduke, feeling the importance of informing the king that he had crossed the river and was pressing on the Parliamentarians, ordered Colonel Shakerley to convey his message as speedily as possible. Shakerley, to avoid the long circuit by Holt Bridge, galloped to the Dee, took a wooden tub that was used for slaughtering swine—employed "a batting-staff, used for batting of coarse linen," as an oar—put his servant into this strange boat, his horse swimming by him as he crossed the river—left his servant with the tub—rode to the king, and returned the same way. This speedy intelligence was, through the unhappy blundering of that day, made of no avail. Such an adventure, however, ought not to be forgotten by an annalist of the Dee. The exact place where the adventure occurred does not seem to be known, but it cannot have been far from Eaton; for it is stated in the narrative that the boats at Eaton were then useless, and could not be employed for crossing the river in this emergency.

Eccleston Ferry: from Eaton Park.

We are now brought to the immediate neighbourhood of Chester; but before we turn to the bridges of the city, two points which are close to us should be very definitely marked. These are Aldford, where the Roman pavement of the "Old Ford" may still sometimes be discerned at the bottom of the river; and the ferry at Eccleston, which is well seen from a seat in the Duke of Westminster's park, once a familiar haunt of Richard Wilson, the Artist.

IX.

THE ESTUARY.

THE OLD DEE BRIDGE AT CHESTER—LAND REDEEMED FROM THE SEA—THE WELSH SHORE OF THE ESTUARY—FLINT CASTLE AND HENRY IV.—MOSTYN CASTLE AND HENRY VII.— HOLYWELL AND BASINGWERK—THE COAST OF WIRRALL—SHOTWICK AND BURTON— BISHOP WILSON—IRISH EXPEDITION OF WILLIAM III.

FOLLOWING in due sequence what has been said concerning the Bridges, Fords, and Ferries of the Dee, and being now arrived at the point where the Estuary of the river may correctly be considered to begin, we find our attention arrested in the city of Chester itself at the Old Dee Bridge. We must not indeed pass altogether without notice—above the bend of the river—the light suspension bridge for foot-passengers, which, viewed in combination with pleasure-boats on a broad expanse of water, or with the tower of St. John's Church and the foliage below, has considerable beauty. Still less must we neglect —below this bend—the fine span of the single arch, named the Grosvenor Bridge, which stands at one end of the broad green level of the Roodee, while the other is occupied by the railway-viaduct. Archæology, however, requires that we give our chief thoughts to the ancient structure, which, near the flour-mills and the "Causeway," crosses the river precisely at the bend. These arches have an inestimable value, because, in common with the Cathedral and the older Churches and the City Walls, they visibly connect Chester

I

with the Middle Ages, though, like those other buildings, they have
undergone reparation at various dates. The exact time when this
bridge was built we do not know; and it seems to have been the
successor of a ferry, by which the city used to be entered at the

The Old Bridge : Low Water.

"Ship-Gate." But for many long years it has been intimately
connected with all the military, ecclesiastical, and municipal history
of the good city of Chester.

It has just been said that the Estuary of the Dee may correctly
be regarded as beginning here. This, indeed, is not visibly the

case at the present day. The recovery within the last century and a half of a large extent of land from the salt water has confined the river within a narrow, formal, and artificial channel; and this continues for several miles. The elevated bank on the right side of the stream, called "the Cop," where on fine summer mornings the fresh sea air can be thoroughly enjoyed, reminds us of Holland, except indeed that full in view, beyond the iron-works of Saltney, are the Welsh hills which form the nearer boundary of the Vale of Clwyd, with Moel Fammau conspicuous as the highest point. It is to be observed further that this walk along the river-side brings us very speedily over the Cheshire border. The Dee, for some short distance, is again entirely a Welsh river. Flintshire claims once more a consider- able area on its right bank, as we saw that it did in an earlier part of its course; and the large parish of Hawarden roams over the new level land to a point near the very walls

Grosvenor Bridge at Chester.

of Chester. A similar redeeming of useful ground from the sea-tide will no doubt be continued, from time to time, further down the Dee; but at present, eight miles below Chester, the river widens out suddenly and becomes a visible estuary.

From this point we have to deal with a Welsh shore and an English shore as two very distinct subjects, and separated from one another by broad sands or a broad tide; and it is somewhat difficult, within the small space at our command, to decide in what order to take the topics which suggest themselves on the right hand and on the left. A decision must be made on the moment; and perhaps no method will be more convenient than first to glance at the points of interest on the Welsh shore, and then to cross to the English, and finally, from the farthest corner of the latter, where it touches

View of Chester from the Cop.

the open sea, to look across the broadening expanse of water to the receding mountains of Wales again.

The points of interest on the Welsh shore in connection with history are easily named. They are Flint and Mostyn, with Holywell and Basingwerk between them.

The Castles of Flint and Mostyn are associated, in a very animated

manner, with two of the most critical moments in the history of the
English monarchy—the accession of Henry IV. and the accession of
Henry VII. As to the town of Flint, no place can be more unin-
teresting. It stands low, and has a dingy, gritty character, very
discouraging to the tourist who comes to the place with his mind
full of its ancient fame. But the ruined fortress stands out boldly
on the very edge of the sand, in sufficient strength to remind us
of Shakspeare's words con-
cerning "the rude ribs of that
ancient castle" — "the limits
of yon lime and stone" within
which, for the last time,
Richard was "contained" a
king. An incident occurred
at the interview between him
and Bolingbroke which is well
worth quoting again from the
pages of Froissart, though it
has often been quoted before.
It is one of those strange
instances which we cannot
explain, of the sympathy
sometimes shown by the animal creation with man in
times of great change. The

Flint Castle, and Estuary of the Dee.

king had a greyhound to
which he was much attached, and which was in the habit of recog-
nising no one else. Whilst he and the Duke of Lancaster were
discoursing in the courtyard, this creature, which used to leap upon
the former, came to the latter, "and made to hym the same frendly
countinaunce and chere as he was wonte to do to the kynge. The
duke, who knewe not the grayhounde, demanded of the kynge what
the grayhounde wolde do. 'Cosyn,' quod the kynge, 'it is a greit

good token to you, and an evyll sygne to me.' 'Sir, howe knowe
you that?' quod the duke. 'I know it well,' quod the kynge. 'The
grayhounde maketh you chere this daye as kynge of Englande, as
ye shalbe, and I shalbe deposed. The grayhounde hath this knowledge naturallye; therefore take hym to you; he wyll folowe you
and forsake me.'" It is needless to remind the reader how the
political history to which this incident belongs connects itself
with Owen Glendower, and so with almost the whole course of
the Dee.

The name of another noted Welshman, Owen Tudor, forms the
natural introduction to a correlative incident in the annals of English
Monarchy, which took place at Mostyn Castle. It seems that his
grandson, Henry of Richmond, passed much of his time in Wales,
after his disappearance from Brittany. On one occasion he had a
narrow escape at Mostyn. The story may be given in the words of
Pennant—partly because his own residence was in this very part
of Flintshire, where, as he says, "its northern side is washed by
the estuary of the Dee"—partly because he is himself the prince of
Welsh antiquarians. "While the Earl of Richmond was at Mostyn,
a party attached to Richard III. arrived there to apprehend him.
He was then about to dine; but had just time to leap out of a back
window, and make his escape through a hole, which to this day is
called the King's. Richard-ap-Howel, then lord of Mostyn, joined
Henry at the battle of Bosworth, and, after the victory, received
from the king, in token of gratitude for his preservation, the belt and
sword he wore on that day; he also pressed Richard greatly to follow
him to Court; but he nobly answered, like the Shunammitish woman,
'*I dwell among mine own people.*'"

Mostyn is near the place where the river shore becomes the sea-
coast and the estuary finally ceases. Flint is near the place where
the estuary visibly begins, the Dee stretching out a sudden surface
of sand to a great breadth, immediately on being extricated from
the artificial restraint which has been mentioned above. About

halfway between these two castles, and nearly side by side, are the ruins of Basingwerk Abbey and St. Winifred's celebrated fountain at Holywell. Each of them deserves very careful attention, particularly the latter, both because of the beautiful architecture of its church, and because of the half-poetical, half-superstitious feeling which still lingers about the place. And occasion must be taken in our concluding chapter for some further reference to these subjects, as well as to other matters connected with this bank of the Dee, especially the salmon in its water, and the lead above its shore. At present justice requires that we cross over to the English bank and devote three short paragraphs to that.

In the British coast there is no more remarkable feature than the long square-ended peninsula, called Wirrall, which divides the Mersey from the Dee. And if this feature is remarkable in reference to the general English coast, it is not less so when considered

Shotwick Church : Norman Arch.

in reference to the shape of the county of Cheshire, which might be compared to a shallow cup having two handles, one projecting far eastward into the mountains of Derbyshire, the other jutting out, as we have seen, between two parallel rivers. This last peculiarity of Wirrall, Drayton has seized with his usual accuracy. It is particularly in reference to this part of the course of the Dee that the fitness of the following address to Cheshire is seen :—

> " O thou thrice happy shire, confinèd so to be
> 'Twixt two such famous floods, as Mersey is and Dee.
> The Dee, upon the West, from Wales doth thee divide ;
> The Mersey, on the North, from the Lancastrian side,
> Thy natural sister-shire, and linkt unto thee so
> That Lancashire along with Cheshire still doth go."

If the county of Cheshire were our subject, it would be necessary to give consideration to this great interfluvial peninsula as a whole : and physical changes so remarkable have taken place here, and there has seemed to some so great a likelihood of further changes, that our geographical bard has reason for marking well the place—

> " Where Mersey for more state,
> Assuming broader banks, himself so proudly bears,
> That at his stern approach extended Wyrrall fears
> That (what betwixt his floods of Mersey and the Dee)
> In very little time devourèd he might be."

Our concern is merely with the shore of Wirrall on the side of the Dee : yet even there some subjects of interest must wait, as in the case of the Welsh shore, for our gathering up of fragments at the last. Here, as we move on to the final opening of the river into the sea on its English side, just one biographical and one historical topic may be noticed.

Where the estuary begins to spread into its broad expanse—not far from Shotwick, whose little church preserves in its surviving Norman arch a reminiscence of the forcible ecclesiastical sway that extended over this region soon after the Conquest—in the pleasing village of Burton was born, in a lowly home, but "of honest parents, fearing God," as he says in his Diary, a bishop of the modern English Church, whose example is full of the noblest lessons. On a little escarpment of rock, which is ascended by steps, stands the school in which Thomas Wilson was educated. After having graduated at Trinity College, Dublin, he became curate at Winwick to his uncle, Dr. Sherlock, and finally he was made, by

Lord Derby, Bishop of Sodor and Man, in which post he died, at the age of ninety-three, in 1755, after having held the see fifty-eight years. An English bishopric was offered to him more than once; but through his great attachment to the inhabitants of the Isle of Man he refused. We are told that "Cardinal Fleury wanted much to see him, and sent over on purpose to inquire after his health, his age, and the date of his consecration, as they were the two oldest bishops, and, he believed, the poorest in Europe; at the same time inviting him to France. The Bishop sent the Cardinal an answer, which gave him so high an opinion of him, that he obtained an order that no French privateer should ravage the Isle of Man. Mr. Keble, in his biography of Bishop Wilson, remarks that Cardinal Fleury must have recollected the instinctive forbearance of Marlborough, when the demesnes of Cambray were at his mercy, and when, out of reverence to Fénélon, no farm upon them was plundered; and he beauti-

School at Burton.

fully adds: "These two passages taken together form one of those bright and pleasant gleams, too rare, alas! in history, when one age or country makes a signal for good to another far away, and the answer comes promptly and cheerfully."

When Wilson was a very young man, there was unwonted commotion on the Wirrall shore of the Dee, not far below Burton; for here, at Parkgate, the flotilla of William III. was assembled before he went across the channel to fight the Battle of the Boyne. It must never be forgotten that, up to that period, the customary line of communication between London and Ireland passed by Chester and the Dee: but this topic will be resumed in connection with a pathetic passage in the life of Milton.

The Dee from above Burton.

X.*

HALLS AND CASTLES ON THE DEE.

THE RIVER RETRACED FROM ITS MOUTH — THE WELSH SIDE — MOSTYN HALL — HALKIN CASTLE — THE ROAD BY NORTHUP — UPPER SOUGHTON HALL — EWLOE CASTLE AND HENRY II. — HAWARDEN CASTLE AND PARK — CHESTER — NEW EPISCOPAL PALACE — AVENUES IN EATON PARK — EATON HALL — PLAN OF THE NEW BUILDINGS — RELATION OF THE PARK TO THE DEE.

HE present subject will occupy two chapters, and it has been considered best to commence from the mouth of the Dee, working upwards to the source. The breaking point will be Eaton. Of course in so short a compass many interesting and beautiful places must be passed by without even a notice, and many of those that are described will have far too short a space; indeed, there are no fewer than six mansions that would form interesting subjects for the two papers devoted to the whole number.

On the Cheshire bank of the Dee there is a long sweeping *plateau*, extending from West Kirby to Shotwick, which is studded with mansions and villas, occupied in some instances by the families who have for many years been lords of the soil; but in still more by wealthy merchants, who have chosen this part of Cheshire for a residence. The road on the crest of this rising ground is very beautiful, and the slope to the Estuary of the Dee seems to point it out as being peculiarly fitted for pleasant grounds and undulating

---

* This chapter, and the following, are written by Mr. Rimmer. See the Preface.

parks; but the historical interest of the Estuary of the Dee principally centres on spots upon the Welsh side.

Mostyn Hall is the first mansion on the right hand side of the
river, sailing up from the sea. It is the seat of Lord Mostyn, and
is in a large and well-wooded park stocked with deer. It was built

Mostyn Hall.

originally about the year 1420, but it has been altered into a fine
country-residence, without, it is pleasant to be able to add, losing all
of its venerable appearance. It is approached by a magnificent
entrance called Porth Mawr, and a long avenue of fine forest trees
of various kinds.

The pedigree of this family occupies nearly fifty feet of parchment, and is shown to visitors ; and there is also in the house a valuable collection of armour, old heirlooms of the family.

When Henry Tudor, Earl of Richmond, was born, he was not a probable heir to the throne of England: he was a grandson of Owen Tudor, and descended, by his mother, from John of Gaunt. He had been brought up in the court of the Duke of Bretagne, and would, one might think, have been hardly worth the notice of King Richard III. ; and yet the latter tried to inveigle him to England, having a sort of instinctive fear of him :

> " I do remember me—Henry the Sixth
> Did prophesy that Richmond should be king,
> When Richmond was a little peevish boy."

And again he says to Buckingham,

> " Richmond ! when last I was in Exeter
> The mayor in courtesy show'd me the castle,
> And called it Rougemont—at which name I started,
> Because a bard of Ireland told me once
> I should not live long after I saw Richmond."

The earl took refuge here, for he thought the Welsh blood in him would secure a goodly following from the Principality, and, as before has been mentioned, was closely pursued by Richard, only escaping with difficulty.

At Mostyn Hall is a silver harp that has been in the family for more than three centuries, and there is also a golden *torque*, which was found at Harlech Castle, about sixty miles distant, and was at one time worn by the Princes of Wales. There is a library here of old British history, and Welsh manuscripts, which, to any one acquainted with the language, would furnish much interesting information of the period of Owen Glendower. This library was taken from Gloddaeth, a fine Elizabethan mansion erected by Sir Roger Mostyn in 1560, and situated about twenty-five miles distant, near the coast. The Mostyn testimonial is a silver candelabrum, and is shown to visitors; it weighs above a hundredweight.

The upper road from Mostyn passes through Holywell and Northup, commanding splendid views of the estuary of the Dee.

Halkin Castle.

Before arriving, however, at the latter place, we reach Halkin Castle, an occasional seat of the Duke of Westminster. It is a formal castellated pile of buildings, in the style which was introduced in the beginning of this century; the situation, however, is very fine, and the grounds are beautiful.

The road from Halkin passes through Northup, and is one of the finest in Wales, increasing in beauty till it reaches Hawarden. Northup Church lies low, but its tall tower is seen at considerable distances from various sides. The tower is apparently of the time of Henry IV., and is encircled with strongly defined bands of cusped work, which give it a distinctive character, yet have a good general effect. The country is undulating and highly cultivated, and studded with broad tall trees. In some parts of the road oaks meet overhead for long distances, and through the stems the charming landscape is continually altering. There is a strong resemblance at high water between this road and some of the lake scenes, while at low water the fields of wheat and hay melt away in the distance into vast flat sandbanks.

Upper Soughton Hall, here delineated, lies close to Northup, and is the residence of Mr. R. Howard ; near it is Soughton Hall, but this does not lie exactly within sight of the Dee. It is, however, a place of great

Upper Soughton Hall.

interest, and is the residence of Mr. Scott-Bankes, who is a lineal descendant of Sir John Bankes, Lord Chief Justice of Common Pleas in the time of Charles I. This family possesses the well-known blacklead mines in Cumberland, and a member of it will be long recollected as the advocate of the British Museum in the House of Commons, and also as the author of the " Civil and Constitutional History of Rome to the Age of Augustus."

Ewloe Castle is an ancient fortress on the road between Northup and Hawarden. Very little is known of its history, but it seems to have been a place of great strength; the walls that remain are eight feet in thickness and of most excellent masonry; there is a staircase in the centre of one of the walls which is shown here. This ruin is not very easily found, being situated in a deep gloomy dell, which bears in its foliage and ruggedness a singular resemblance to a forest-glen in Lower Canada.

Gateway in Ewloe Castle : Entrance to Stair in Wall.

Ewloe contributes its small share to English history. Henry II., notwithstanding his prudence and justice, found his crown but a "polished perturbation :" for besides his family-troubles, enemies rose up in the north and the south, in the east and in Wales, and his army was drawn into the Glen at Ewloe by David and Conan, the sons of Owen Gwynedd, where it was defeated with frightful slaughter : and, indeed, no one can see the place without being struck by the hopeless case which an army shut up as this was, must have been in. The small brook at the bottom of the defile is called Wepre Brook, and it runs into the grounds of Wepre Hall, an old-fashioned residence overlooking the estuary of the Dee.

Hawarden Castle is the seat of the Rt. Hon. W. E. Gladstone, whose son inherited it from Sir Stephen Glynne, Bart., his maternal uncle. It is built in the castellated style, and resembles Halkin to some extent in general appearance; perhaps it is less formal, but at the date of its design, 1809, the laudable attempt to restore our

Hawarden Castle.

national architecture was in its infancy, and all buildings of that period look crude to modern eyes. Indeed, the progress that has been made in this style, even in the last twelve years, is astonishing; and some recent domestic buildings fully equal the Tudor homes of the sixteenth century. The word "domestic" is used advisedly, for during this same period church-architecture has sadly lagged

K

behind; there is a stereotyped character about it that would enable
any one to predict with tolerable certainty what the appearance of
any church would be of which the dimensions, the cost, and the
period of the architecture were given.*

Hawarden Park is not exceeded in beauty by any demesne in the
world. It much resembles Arundel, but the views from an ancient
castle in the middle of it are more varied and extensive, and much
finer. The branches of one enormous oak-tree sweep on the ground
on every side, and form a sort of canopy, through which the landscape is seen as through intricate tracery. The counties of Caer-
narvon, Denbigh, Flint, Cheshire, and Lancashire appear from the
old castle like a vast ordnance map rolled out. The castle is a very
noble ruin; and one cannot but regret that other old monuments
were not enclosed in private or public parks where they would
be as well cared for. It appears to belong to the middle of the
thirteenth century, and has many examples of the square cusped
arch which, with one or two other peculiarities, seem to point it out
as having been designed by some one from the southern counties.

The road from Hawarden to Boughton is exceedingly grand; a
vast sweep of country, quite unsurpassed in richness, leads down to
the Dee, and spreads itself on the Cheshire side: sixty square miles
of smiling fields and pasture are within easy sight, and these are
delightfully diversified with elms and sycamores, while here and
there are tall formal rows of Lombardy poplars. From any part of
this road the termination of the estuary of the Dee is visible, and
few, who only know it from maps as a wedge-shaped bay, covering
some forty-eight square miles, would recognise it at low water, when
it becomes a vast sandbank, through which the Dee seems to trickle
like a little feeble brook. Much of this land may yet be reclaimed,
as many hundred acres were by an ancestor of Sir Stephen Glynne.

Hawarden Castle formerly belonged to the Stanley family, the

---

* Since the first edition of this work great progress has been made in church
architecture.—A.R.

last possessor being the Lord Derby who was so arbitrarily executed at Bolton, and it was purchased by Mr. Serjeant Glynne, afterwards Lord Chief Justice ; but so fairly does he seem to have acted in his high office, that he held it during the Restoration and was knighted by King Charles II.

As we sail up the Dee, past Queen's Ferry, we soon arrive at Chester, and find but little fairly connected with the present subject that can arrest our attention. The Bishop's Palace is a large brick building, delightfully situated on the river. The Ecclesiastical Commissioners recently built it, in place of the old one in Abbey Square, which, though interesting from its old associations, had only a little more architectural merit to recommend it than the present one. Opposite the present palace, on the other side of the Dee, is the residence of Sir Thomas Frost, and next to it that of his brother. They are pleasing houses, in small but neat grounds. As we advance up the river, towards Eaton, we pass Boughton,

Bishop's Palace, Chester.

where there are many agreeable residences, and arrive at Heron Bridge, the seat of Mr. Charles Potts, shown in the engraving. It is one of the most charming spots on the Dee, and is embedded in tall elms and beech-trees. Near to this is Netherlegh House, until

lately belonging to the Cotgreave family, of Chester, now extinct;
and in the grounds are the remains of Chester Cross,* removed here
early in this century.

The Eaton woods are now reached, and just beyond Netherlegh

Heron Bridge.

was one of the park lodges, an octagonal building, overshadowed
with enormous trees. This lodge was burned down soon after the
publication of the first edition of this work.

* This cross formed the subject of a notice in the *Art Journal* for April, 1873.

Eaton Hall, the Cheshire seat of the Duke of Westminster, is situated in a very large, though hardly picturesque park, which is liberally thrown open to strangers, and, in consequence, is a great

Eaton Hall.

boon to Chester. The Grosvenor Lodge is only a few hundred yards from the city walls, and an avenue of two miles in length leads up to the deer-park, which is entered by a large lodge and gateway, and into which the public are freely admitted. The Hall is a mile farther on in the park, and directly in front of the gates is the Wrexham avenue of two miles in length, bordered on each side by great forest-trees. This avenue leads to a farmhouse called Belgrave; and perhaps few persons who have not been here know the origin of that now famous name. Another avenue of about the same length leads to Pulford, where one of the ancient lodges still remains; while another of about a mile in length leads to the beautiful village of Aldford—the old Roman ford over the river, alluded to before. The Hall itself has now been entirely rebuilt in the style which prevailed in France during the fifteenth and sixteenth centuries, and which the architect has been prominent in adopting in England— and greatly modifying to suit present requirements. The general effect is very grand, and has only been apparent since the removal of the scaffolding. A tower of about a hundred and seventy feet high over the chapel unites all the parts together. The plan of the mansion is simply beautiful; indeed, there is not a house in England built on a more perfect arrangement. The temptation is strong to describe it, especially as it can be understood without even a drawing.

The hall is an octagonal room in the centre of the house, about seventy-five feet in length and from thirty to forty broad; on each side of this hall, at the end farthest from the entrance, are two doors leading into ante-rooms—one the ante-drawing-room and the other the ante-dining-room; each is lit by three large windows, and is thirty-three feet in length; they are fine rooms in themselves, and well-proportioned. From these lead the drawing-room and the dining-room respectively—both exceedingly grand rooms. But this is not what we have to do with; all we are discussing now is the plan of the house. These rooms, which are ingenious in design and shape, have each two oriel windows, and are lighted by three others and a large bay window: this suite completes the east side. The south is occupied by the end of the drawing-room and a vast library —all *en suite*. The library is lighted by four bay-windows, three

Eaton Hall, from the Aldford Road.

flat ones, and a fine alcove, and the rest of the main building to the
west is made up of billiard and smoking-rooms, waiting-hall, groom
of chamber's sitting and bed-rooms, and a carpet-room—besides the
necessary staircases.   This completes the main building, and a
corridor leads to the kitchen and cooks' offices; this corridor, which
passes over the upper part of the kitchen, branches off into two parts,
one leading to an excellently planned mansion for the family and the
private secretary, and another leading to the stables, which are
arranged with great skill.   The pony stable, the carriage-horse
stable, the riding-horses, occupy different sides; and through these
are arranged, just in the right places, the rooms for livery, and
saddle-grooms, and coachmen. The laundry, washhouse, gunroom,
and game-larder, occupy another building, which, however, is easily
approached; and the whole building, though it extends seven
hundred feet in length, is a perfect model of compactness.   Great
facilities are given to any one who desires to see it.

Returning to the park at Grosvenor Lodge, that we may follow
the Dee from thence, we pass by Boughton, joining the park again
at Eccleston, an extremely beautiful village.   The river skirts it as
far as Poulton, where it finally leaves it.   The rectory at Eccleston
stands in pleasant grounds surrounded by Eaton park, and is very
characteristic of English scenery.   The grounds slope down to the
Dee, and are delightfully studded with trees.   All the length of the
Dee, from the time it passes Grosvenor Lodge to the time it finally
leaves the park, is seven miles.

XI.*

HALLS AND CASTLES ON THE DEE.

SAIGHTON TOWER—JUNCTION OF THE ALYN—COURSE OF THE DEE BELOW OVERTON—ACTON
HALL AND JUDGE JEFFREYS—ENGLISH AND CLASSICAL ARCHITECTURE—BRYN-Y-PYS—
ERBISTOCK — KNOLTON HALL—WYNNESTAY—INSTRUCTIONS TO A CHAPLAIN—CHIRK
CASTLE — PLAS MADOC — PLAS NEWYDD — A WELSH BARD'S DESCRIPTION OF OWEN
GLENDOWER'S HALL.

PPOSITE Eaton, and about two miles from the river, is
Saighton Tower, formerly a country residence of the
abbots of Chester. Though considerably altered, it retains
much of its original character. Saighton Manor was
held by the secular canons of St. Werburgh before the Conquest, and
they retained it at the time of the Domesday survey. The present
building was erected at the latter end of the fifteenth century by
Simon Ripley, and is a very interesting specimen of the domestic
architecture of the period. It has been clumsily restored of late,
and the unsightly crow-step gables, as they are commonly called,
have been added, as shown in the annexed drawing; but in the year
1817 it was engraved for Ormerod's " Cheshire," and a very beautiful
drawing of it is preserved in that work, where it is shown in its
ancient form. Almost the only part of it which remains in its
entirety is the central tower or entrance. The site of it is very
delightful, and it commands a fine view of the Cheshire hills.

* This chapter, and the preceding, are written by Mr. Rimmer. See the Preface.

The river presents no very remarkable features as we ascend it from this point, until we arrive at Overton. It winds about considerably, and receives as a tributary the beautiful river Alyn, which runs through the vale of Gresford, in which are some of the most charming residences in Wales; one especially, called Trevallyn Old Hall, with pointed gables and great stacks of chimneys, standing in a small but finely wooded park, is a very model of an English home.

Saighton Tower.

From the junction of the Alyn with the Dee up to Overton, the river runs through clay banks, and the scenery along it is very tame; the distance in a straight line is not above seven miles, but the sinuosities of its course make its actual length about twice this distance. Near Bangor is Emral Hall, not occupied, and belonging to Sir Richard Puleston. Gredington Hall, the seat of Lord Kenyon; and Hanmer, and Bettisfield, both residences of Lord Hanmer, are not far away.

Acton Hall is the beautiful residence of Sir Robert Cunliffe, M.P., and is situated in a very noble park, which is well wooded. It is remarkable for having been the birthplace of Judge Jeffreys, of notorious memory, of whom Lord Campbell, in his "Lives of the Lord Chancellors," has made the following memorable statement. He declares that he undertook to write his biography with a sort of conviction that an infamous name had clung to him without quite sufficient cause; he had a strong impression that with all his faults he must have some redeeming feature in his character, and that his would be the grateful task to make the most of it, and stave off a little at least of the obloquy and almost terror that surround his name; but he declares, after his work was over, that he does not find one single plea he can urge in palliation of the universal detestation in which his memory has been held from his own times even to the present day.

Between Acton and the Dee lies the pleasant estate of Gerwyn, the seat of Mr. Peel, a nephew of the late Premier; and on the other side of the river is the delightful residence of Mr. Edmund Peel, the principal landowner in this district. The park skirts the highway for nearly two miles, and is only separated from it by an open iron railing, which enables passers-by to enjoy the prospect of spreading oaks and undulating grass-slopes. The style of this house is Italian, and its colour is a warm ochre, slightly inclining to buff.

In the divers discussions that occur continually among the rival candidates for the various styles of architecture, it must be admitted that the advocates of English architecture have had quite the better of it. Indeed, for city and commercial purposes, the style which prevailed in our country during the fifteenth and sixteenth centuries is unquestionably the most effective and the most economical. This is perhaps generally admitted; while, as to ecclesiastical purposes of course there can be but one opinion. But it may be well not to lose sight entirely of this consideration. There is always great beauty in an Italian mansion when of good colour and in a proper situation. The eye finds a broad, flat space to rest upon; and if the colour of the building is sufficiently subdued, the elms and oaks of a park will supply outline, and depth, and variety. Indeed, with every feeling most strongly pronounced in favour of English architecture, such as the kind which prevailed some hundred years before Elizabeth, it must frankly be said we are too apt to do injustice to classic styles. In a city they are out of place, and one passes by a Greek façade with a feeling of chill. Perhaps a better illustration of this could hardly be found than the commonly known example of the "Temple on the Ilissus." It is, as need hardly be said, an Ionic building, with four columns in the gable front, all affirmed—and perhaps correctly so—to be perfect examples of the Greek Ionic style. Now it is more than probable that it exactly suited the rugged scenery it

Bryn-y-Pys.

was designed for, and indeed stood out like a gem; those who had the privilege of seeing it in its entirety (for it has recently been destroyed) always said that such was its character. And the same remarks might easily apply to the Doric Portico which has been so often illustrated in early architectural books, and is called the

"Gate of the Agora : " for this undoubtedly stood well among the rugged cliffs of the Acropolis, being a perfect example of a cold, calm, lifeless front. Well, perhaps few persons would easily suppose that these two celebrated porticos are precisely identical with the dreary fronts of the great number of chapels of many denominations that stand back some few yards from the long lines of brick houses and shops in most of the large English towns—identical, because the stereotyped and easy form is given in joiners' guides. These reflections occur from a slight examination of the front of Bryn-y-Pys. It is a very excellent example of a quiet Italian building, without pretentiousness, and is charmingly situated on an eminence of a well-timbered park. But all this is opening up a wide, and perhaps somewhat collateral subject.

On the opposite side of the river from Bryn-y-Pys is Rose Hill, a pleasant mansion; its park joins that of Erbistock. The Dee skirts along them for nearly a mile; and some of the scenes upon it, especially near Rose Hill, are among the most beautiful in Wales. On the other side of the river again is a pleasant house called Overton Cottage, and of this, as of the two others last mentioned, it is satisfactory to say that no attempt at architectural effect has marred the quiet beauty of the landscape. A road goes above it at the back, from which there is a lovely scene, the house and its plantations and walks filling in a bend of the river.

At Erbistock is a ferry, an illustration of which appears in Chapter VIII., and a church, which has recently been modernised. There is, unfortunately, a high roof which shows its sides to the river above the trees, and is the only part of the church that is visible. It has not a very pleasant effect in the landscape. High roofs, if well managed, are good ; but very commonly a chapel with low walls is overwhelmed with a vast acreage of roof that becomes the sole feature. It may be taken as a general rule, that except with peculiar and very skilful treatment, a high-pitched roof requires high walls to rest on.

Knolton Hall is near this, and has been altered with much taste by Mr. R. C. Cotton, the late proprietor, a brother of Lord Combermere, who immortalised himself in the Peninsular War. The front of Knolton is in black and white, after the fashion of so many houses in the south of Cheshire and Shropshire. It was a kind of

Knolton Hall.

large farm-house when Mr. Cotton purchased the estate; and perhaps it seemed to offer no very promising opportunity of being transformed into a country residence; but this has been done very effectively, and a valuable specimen of antiquity is preserved to the country. The entrance-hall is large, and peculiarly happy in its transformation.

Knolton Hall was once visited by Cromwell, who stayed for some little time there, and is said to have greatly fancied it for a residence. The Dee skirts the woods for about a mile, and a footpath has been cut through them from whence there are many beautiful views of the country. This part of the river is certainly the most pleasing, more so now than Llangollen, which, with its railway stations and mines and quarries, has lost some of its beauty. But soon after leaving Llangollen we re-enter the ancient charms of the valley.

Pen-y-llan is the only residence of importance until we reach Wynnestay, the magnificent seat of Sir Watkin Williams Wynn, the largest landowner in Wales. Wynnestay was formerly the residence of Madoc ap Gryffydd Maeler, who founded Valle Crucis Abbey. It came into possession of the Wynns by the intermarriage of one of the Gwedyr family of that name with the heiress of Eyton Evans. It is surrounded by a wall of about eight miles in length, and there are many herds of deer in the beautiful park.

The old Hall was unfortunately burned down in 1858, and a vast collection of valuable heirlooms, many of which had a national interest, was destroyed. The following is the description given of it by Pennant about eighty years ago:—"The house has been built at various times. The most ancient part is a gateway of wood and plaster, dated 1616. On a tower within the court is this excellent distich, allusive to the name of the house: Wynne stay, or rest satisfied with the good things providence has so liberally showered on you.

> "Cui domus est victusque decens, cui patria dulcis,
> Sunt satis hæc vitæ, cætera cura labor."

The new part, built by the first Sir Watkin, is of itself a good house, yet was only a portion of a more extensive design. It is finished in that honest, substantial, yet neat manner becoming the seat of an English country gentleman, adapted to the reception of his worthy neighbours, who may experience his hospitality without dread of spoiling his frippery ornaments, becoming only the assembly-rooms of a town house or the villa of a great city." What Pennant would have thought of the present house it is impossible to say; the interior is exceedingly splendid, and the exterior may be described as a rather severe adaptation of the Louis Quatorze style. It was finished by the late baronet at an enormous cost.

Avenue and Principal Entrance, Wynnestay.

The avenue from Ruabon forms here the subject of an engraving, and is about a mile in length, or perhaps a little more. It leads almost from the gates of the old church, in which are many monuments of the Wynn family, including also the first of the family who left Gwyder to settle here. The father of this one, who died in 1678, has left behind him a letter of instructions to his chaplain, conveying so simple a picture of the relations which a country gentleman then bore to his chaplain that the temptation is strong to introduce it.

"First you shall have the chamber I showed you in my gate, private to yourself, with lock and key and all necessaries. In the morning I expect you should rise and say prayers in my hall to my household below before they go to work, and when they come in at nyght; that you call before you all the workmen, specially to give and take accompt of them, of their belief, and of what Sir Meredith taught them. I beg you to continue for the most part in the lower house : you are to have only what is done there, that you may inform me of any disorder there ; there is a baylif of husbandry and a porter, who will be commanded by you. The mornings after you be up, and said prayers as afore, I wo^d you to bestow in study, or any commendable exercise of your body.

"Before dinner you are to come up and attend grace, or prayers if there be any publicke ; and to set up if there be not greater stranger above the chyldren—who you are to teach in y^r own chamber. When the table from half downwards is taken up, then you are to rise and to walk in the alleys near at hand until grace time, and to come in then for that purpose.

"After dinner, if I be busy, you may go to bowles, shuffel board, or any other honest decent recreation till I go abroad. If you see me voyd of business, and go to ride abroad, you shall command a horse to be made ready for you by the grooms of the stable, and to go with me. If I go to bowles or shuffel board, I shall lyke of your company if the place be not made up with strangers. I would have you go every Sunday in the year to some church hereabouts to preache, giving warning to the parish to bring the yowths at afternoon in the church to be catekysed, in which point is my greatest care that you be paynfull and dilygent. Avoyd the ale-house, to sytt and keepe drunkards company there, being the greatest discredit your function can have." The simplicity and arrogance of this document are charming, and bring to view more vividly the real position of landlord and chaplain than anything that even Macaulay has handed down to us in his History of England.

There is another seat of Sir Watkin Williams Wynn on Bala Lake, which is perhaps more a luxurious shooting-box than a country mansion. Its grounds skirt the lake for some distance, and a drawing of it has already appeared in the chapter on Bala Lake.

Chirk Castle lies a little off the Dee, and is a place of very great interest. It was originally founded in the early part of the eleventh

L

Wynnestay.

century, and has for many years been the residence of the family of Myddleton. Hugh Myddleton, who projected the New River scheme from Hertford to London, was a brother of the first Sir Thomas. The family has since assumed the name of Biddulph. There are very many interesting portraits in the house, and among others a full-length of Oliver Cromwell.

Near this place is Brynkinalt, a seat of Lord Arthur Hill Trevor,

Plas Madoc, formerly the Seat of G. H. Whalley, Esq., M.P.

a relative of the late Duke of Wellington, and here much of the early life of the General was spent. This house is delightfully situated in a well-timbered park, but, as in the case of some others of which mention has been made, its architecture is rather old-fashioned Gothic.

Plas Madoc, which forms the subject of an illustration, was the

L 2

seat of Mr. G. H. Whalley, who took so deep an interest in the "Claimant." It is an exceedingly pleasant residence, but rather spoiled by the great number of collieries that surround it.

Llangollen Valley at first disappoints a visitor who has had his expectations raised by its renowned name, and, though larger and much longer than Gresford Vale, it is hardly so beautiful. Still there are some pleasant scenes in it, especially as we approach nearer to Corwen. Close to the village of Llangollen is the notable Plas Newydd, formerly the residence of Lady E. Butler and the Hon. Miss Ponsonby, who lived to a great age and affected much singularity, both in costume and habits, but succeeded nevertheless in gaining the respect of their neighbours. This house has been extravagantly eulogised, and its fame brought large numbers to its offer by auction, which took place some few years ago ; but it was not found equal to the anticipations of the people.

There are numerous residences along the river as far as Corwen, where we arrive at Rhaggatt, the seat of an ancient Welsh family named Lloyd, who own a large estate on the side of the Dee ; and on the opposite bank was the old Hall of Owen Glendower. A description of it, by a Welsh bard, still remains ; and in his eyes it seemed very splendid, equal in magnificence to what he imagined Westminster must be. It had, he said, nine halls with large wardrobes, no doubt the retainers' apartments. Then there was a wooden house near this, supported on posts, with eight apartments for guests. There was also a church in the form of a cross, and several chapels. "The seat was surrounded with every conveniency for good living," says Pennant, "and every support to hospitality. A park, warren, and pigeon-house, a mill, orchard and vineyard, a fishpond filled with pike and gwyniaids, the last introduced from Bala lake." The vestiges of the house are small. The moat is very apparent. The measurement of the area it enclosed is 46 paces by 26. Glendower had much to apprehend from the neighbouring fortress of Dinas Bran. Rug, pronounced like Reeg, is the residence of one of the Wynn family, to whom it has recently descended; it is near Corwen, and delightfully situated on the Dee. It formerly belonged to the Vaughan family, who are lineally descended from Owen Glendower, and until lately there were many relics of the great Welsh chieftain in the house. Here the Welsh

Llanderval Hall.

king Gryffydd ap Cynan was betrayed into the power of Hugh Lupus, Earl of Chester, and removed to the castle in that city, where he underwent twelve years' imprisonment. On the attainder of Glendower, Rug was sold by Henry IV. to one of the Salusbury family.

Near Bala Lake is Palé Hall, a handsome modern building

situated in a charming park: and it is pleasant to be able to add that it is quite in keeping with all its surroundings. The park is an ancient one, and the house stands on the site of a much older residence. Mr. Henry Robertson, some time M.P. for Shrewsbury, lives here. He was the engineer for the viaduct over the Dee, which has already been noticed.

We have lingered so long on the lower parts of the Dee that there is not much room to describe Rhiwlas (pronounced Roo-las), the residence of the ancient family of Price. This house has lately been rebuilt, and, judging from a distant view of it, it seems to be a very handsome edifice. Pennant records that one of the family of Price was a member for the county in the Long Parliament, but was displaced in consequence of his loyalty to the King.

Many country houses, as before has been said, have been passed by with an imperfect notice; and many more, I am painfully aware, have been omitted entirely; but the aim of these two chapters has been principally to offer a slight sketch of what travellers up the Dee might see without trouble or much delay.

XII.

CONCLUSION.

HE course of a river has often been compared to the course of human life ; and the comparison, even if pressed very closely and in many particulars, is apt and true.

Consider, for example, in each case, the smallness and obscurity of beginning, contrasted with the great place in public attention which may be filled in the end. Among famous rivers one of the most illustrious, though not one of the largest, is the Tiber. An accomplished traveller has recently traced it, and given us his observations and reflections upon it, from the mouth to the source. He was guided by an old shepherd to the spot in which this river rises, through the green sod, and among strawberry blossoms and dwarf willow-herb, in an immense beech forest, where the Apennines, after running some distance eastward, approach nearest to the Adriatic. Here the old shepherd-guide, resting upon his staff, said, *"And this is called the Tiber at Rome."* The traveller adds, most naturally, " It was like being present at the birth of one who should alter and control the destinies of the world."

But we need not suppose ourselves to stand by the cradle of some great man, and to be dreaming over his future history. The most commonplace career of a human life is full of profound and varied interest; and even a commonplace river (not that we can allow the Dee to be so described) may be used to represent that career as in a parable. The variety of incident and of surrounding circumstances, as we travel onward from point to point, constitutes a most striking part of this near resemblance. The contributions of new experience which enter, from this side and that, into the mind and heart of every human being as he grows older, are truly like the affluents which augment and modify the river in its onward flow. Where could we find a better emblem of childhood than in the sparkling laughter and eager haste of the young brook, as it wanders through its early secluded valleys? The parallel is equally just in the dull monotonous flow and the absence of excitement which, after a short space, are almost sure to come—to say nothing (for on the sadder side of the subject we will not dwell) of turbid waters succeeding to those that were fresh and pure. Finally the thought rests, with a continued sense of the fitness of the comparison, upon the widening opportunities of usefulness which come at the last, in the near presence of that solemn future which is a vast and mysterious ocean.

One characteristic of the latest period of life is that it reverts in memory to the circumstances of the past, and becomes garrulous in describing them. True to the comparison which has been suggested, it seems natural, now that our conclusion is nearly reached, that our meditation on the Dee should recall some of the features of its earlier course. This last chapter will be most properly used for gathering together some facts which were previously omitted, and for a fuller attention to certain matters which hitherto have been very lightly touched.

Our obvious method for grouping such things clearly—so far as any method is needful—is to divide the river into its Alpine, Lowland, and Maritime districts. Our best points for definitely marking this threefold division are clearly Ruabon and Chester. Above and immediately below Bala Lake, and through Corwen, and for some little distance beyond Llangollen, the Dee is a mountain river, besides being strictly and exclusively a Welsh river. At the place of its contact with England, in the neighbourhood of Ruabon, it begins to assume new features of scenery, corresponding with the wider and more open range of history which is now connected with its course. Finally, when the stream, after travelling for some miles in a winding channel along these lower levels, reaches Chester, the tide of the sea becomes a daily recurring variation in its life, and the salt air reminds us of the time when its estuary was famous among the harbours of England.

Of the Alpine region of the Dee very little can be said here. If this part of our subject were to be reconsidered fully and at length, two topics would be suggested for separate observation—the course of the valley and the lake. At present it will be enough to re-invite attention to the lake. We must never forget how large a part it plays in reference to the whole character and history of the river. Bala Lake is almost more to the Dee than is the Lake of Geneva to the Rhone, or the Lake of Constance to the Rhine. The aspect of the low gently-rising land round the Mere has been sufficiently described. Bala is not like Grasmere, for instance, with noble mountain forms immediately at hand. Still less could it be likened to the austere grandeur of Wast-Water. Perhaps the English lake that is nearest in general resemblance, as likewise most similar in dimensions, is Hawes-Water, though that also is far superior in natural beauty. Yet there is an unassuming loveliness in Bala Lake, especially as seen in still weather, which cannot possibly be despised; and above all things we are bound to remember that its associations are thoroughly and intensely Welsh. Its annals run up into the dimmest period of history on the one hand; and, on the other, it has its anecdotes and proverbs, current in our own times among the country folk around. When anything is firmly set and complete in all its parts, it is commonly said, "There it is as firm as Bala bell;" and perhaps the mention of this adage may lead to some attempt at explaining it. Another local adage—"Bala has gone and Bala will go"—has received an explanation, and is connected apparently with that tendency in this lake to sudden flooding which was mentioned in the second paper of this work. The town of Bala having formerly been washed away in one of these abrupt floods, there was a prophecy that the same thing would happen again on a certain day and at a certain hour. It was a market-day, and the people stood round on the hillsides to watch the catastrophe. But the hour passed, and nothing had happened: and the people poured into the town; and there never was such buying and selling at any market in Bala. All such stories and proverbs have a true value, if they help us to fix our attention more definitely than before on some feature which is remarkable, and if they place us in sympathy—were it only the sympathy of mere amusement—with well-defined sections of our fellow-men.

Again, on the second or Lowland region of the Dee we must not dwell at very great length, reserving our chief space for the third. The two extremities of this Lowland region may be defined by the palatial residences of Wynnestay and Eaton; which, in fact, is equivalent to what was said before, when Ruabon and Chester were taken as the extreme limits. One view, which is obtained from the southern point of the park of Sir Watkin Williams Wynn, is, on the whole, the most remarkable view in the whole course of the Dee. This is written with the advantage of a very lively recollection of a walk in the early autumn among the woods which environ this bend of the river. The first touch of beautiful decay was just visible on some of the trees. The birds were, of course, silent; and the flowers that remained told us very plainly that the vigour of the year was exhausted. But each season has its own charm ; and, on this occasion, the season was felt to be in harmony with each successive passage in the river's course, as it now rippled over a shallow bed, now lingered deep and dark under fragments of lichen-covered rock, here made space for the cattle on small levels of green pasture, there ran half hid and appeared far off between trees over-

Nant-y-Belan, Wynnestay Park.

hanging closely from either bank. Nor must two incidents of the walk—one recalling the distant past, the other asserting the commanding power of the present, yet both very characteristic of the place where we were—be, by any means, overlooked. While following the path by the side of the stream, we met two men with coracles on their backs, returning towards Overton from a fishing expedition, apparently not very successful, higher up the river. It seemed like an apparition from the time of the ancient Britons. That other apparition which belonged emphatically to our own time, was the presence of the long line of arches of the great railway viaduct in much strength and grandeur, seen suddenly through the foliage among which we were wandering. In the view, to which special allusion has just been made, and which is obtained from a terraced height above the river, this viaduct is one element, and the aqueduct also, slightly visible beyond. But the great feature of the view is the outspread beauty of the woods, among which the stream is embosomed. With such a prospect before us there is always a temptation to make comparisons; and that which came into the mind here was the view of the Wharfe towards Barden Tower. In one sense, indeed, such a comparison is perhaps very useless; for probably as many persons have visited Nant-y-Belan as Bolton Abbey. Still the juxtaposition in thought of two similar scenes is a real help towards the correct appreciation of either.

It will not be forgotten that, over against Wynnestay, which is in Denbighshire, we find, on the right bank of the Dee, a large detached portion of the county of Flint in contact with Shropshire and Cheshire; nor must we overlook the fact that in this region are Bettisfield, the seat of Lord Hanmer, and Gredington, the seat of Lord Kenyon, "containing," to quote from Mr. Murray's excellent Handbook, "a library collected by the distinguished Chief Justice, founder of the family, and portraits of himself and of his contemporary, Lord Thurlow." These houses, indeed, are somewhat remote from the Dee; but Bettisfield at least would hardly repudiate association with this river, if a fair conclusion may be drawn from some spirited lines by the present Lord Hanmer, beginning with the following stanza :—

" By the Elbe and through the Rheinland I've wandered far and wide,
And by the Save with silver tones, proud Danube's queenly bride,
By Arno's banks and Tiber's shore—but never did I see
A river I could match with thine, old Druid-haunted Dee."

It would be impossible to travel down the course of our river without making some allusion to this ancient Flintshire family: for the sister of one of the ancestors of Lord Hanmer was the wife of Owen Glendower; and it seems probable that the marriage took place in Hanmer Church.

The mention of the great mediæval hero of the Dee may be our link of connection with the only other historical allusion on which we can venture before reaching the city of Chester. This reference is made to the celebrated trial, in the Court of Chivalry, between Sir Robert de Grosvenor and Sir Richard de Scrope, on the right to use certain armorial bearings. The trial lasted three years. Probably no more remarkable fact can be adduced to illustrate the passion for heraldic honours in the later Middle Ages, unless it be that other fact, that when it was decided that the Grosvenors might use the same mark as the Scropes, but with the addition of a silver edge, the former proudly declined the questionable honour, and retained merely the "garb," or sheaf of corn, which is familiar to the eye of every one in Chester. One great point of interest, in regard to the trial, is (to repeat what has been already mentioned in an earlier chapter) that Owen Glendower was among the witnesses, along with the poet Chaucer, with Hotspur and John of Gaunt. The elaborate volumes of Sir N. Harris Nicholas, containing all the depositions, might appear to some persons a waste of industry and time; but, as he truly says in his preface, they tend to preserve from oblivion the names of some of the heroes who fought at Cressy and Poictiers.

In passing along those two broad curves in which the river sweeps round the houses and the castle of Chester, it would be quite unnatural not to pause and to enter the city, for another glance at the Rows; and in the present instance it would be disloyal to make no reference to that restoration of the Cathedral, within and without, which is now entering on its concluding period, and that development of the old King's School, which has been successfully completed, and is now an institution of the city.

As regards the Rows, their peculiarity is felt more and more, in
proportion as they are carefully considered : and hence their claim
to be asserted among the honours and curiosities of the Dee cannot
possibly be shaken. In Chapter VII. the partial resemblance to them
in the streets of Berne was adduced. Since those paragraphs were
written, two other partial resemblances, almost more to the purpose,
have come under observation on the Continent. These are at
Utrecht and at Thun. In the Dutch city there is this close simili-
tude to a Row, that stores or shops are found under the two side
footways, but with this startling difference, that the central roadway
is not a street, but a canal. The features of the chief street in the
little Swiss town of Thun, if added to the features of the chief street
in its larger Swiss neighbour, Berne, would really produce that with
which we are familiar in Chester. In the former are side footways,
elevated above the street, with steps at intervals, and with well-
defined shops underneath, but nothing except the sky overhead. In
the latter are covered arcades, with shops on their inner sides, but
with none beneath the foot-passengers, except in one single spot.
For those who have not seen the Chester Rows, or who, having seen
them, have not duly observed their singular character, these comparisons may be of some little use. One thing must be added,
which is more to the honour of Utrecht and Thun than of Chester,
that in the first two instances, and not in the last, foliage is seen in
combination with the houses.

As regards the restoration of the Cathedral of Chester—a subject
very lightly touched in an earlier chapter—it would be impossible,
in describing the River of Chester, not to lay some stress on a work
which has been prominent before the public during the last twenty
years, and which is now far from approaching its conclusion. The
magnitude of the undertaking may be judged of by the fact that,
in 1872, £55,000 had been spent; and a similar sum, at least, would
be required. Of this, £30,000 has been subscribed, and spent. Nor
will the need of this large undertaking be questioned by any one

who recollects the miserably dilapidated state of the fabric previous to 1868. Large sums have been expended on external roofs and the insertion of foundations; and, to turn to what is more conspicuous, but not more essential, the Tower has been completely restored, and the greater part of the Nave, within and without, in addition to the outside of the Lady Chapel and the outside of the Choir. Attention, too, has been given to the interior of the Choir, and to the North-western Tower, where some perplexing architectural problems have received their solution. It is satisfactory to have to record that the Choir has undergone complete structural and ornamental renovation; and the Great South Transept has been at the same time brought into visible architectural combination with the rest of the interior of the Cathedral. The North-western Tower introduces us to another subject.

Boss in Lady Chapel, Chester, showing the Murder of Thomas-à-Becket.

This corner of Chester Cathedral is worthy of peculiar attention, as being one of the surviving parts of the old Norman Church. Here, too, the residence of the old Norman abbots was in close proximity, if not in absolute contact, with the Church itself. After the Reformation this abbatial residence, at the hands of Bishop Keene, received alterations causing great disfigurement, the buttresses outside being choked and obliterated by the wall of his extended dining-room, and some of his apartments being violently intruded into the North-western Tower. The recent change, which has withdrawn the Episcopal Residence of the Diocese to another position, has

led to the determination to use this site of the Old Palace for an
enlarged and reconstructed Cathedral School: and in the course of
preparation for this great educational improvement, correlative im-

Old Episcopal Palace, Chester.

provements in the aspect of the Cathedral, where it faces the Market
Square, have now been secured.

We are now close to the estuary of our river; and a subject

comes here before our thoughts, which can by no means be omitted by any one who pretends to be the annalist of the Dee. We might be sure, even if we had no direct evidence to produce, that the Northern Sea-Kings, who in the early Middle Ages sailed up all rivers in Western Europe, who reigned over all the Western Islands of Scotland, and who with the "*southern*" members of this Atlantic archipelago included in one of their dioceses the Isle of Man, must have made very familiar acquaintance with the Dee. But direct evidence is not wanting. Not only can we quote the "Saxon Chronicle," in its mention of the inroad of Hastings and his expulsion by Alfred, but the names of places can be adduced in permanent attestation of the occupation of this estuary by the Norsemen.

The course of the Dee might be usefully followed on the etymological method, as well as the pictorial or the directly historical. All its higher portion is intensely British, as may be seen by those names on the map, of which only a Welshman can understand the true significance, and which only a Welshman can correctly spell. The intermediate part might furnish, in its local etymology, some interesting and puzzling studies to the learned student who should wish to discriminate its British, Saxon, and Danish elements. Here in the close neighbourhood of the Western Sea we are concerned not with those marks of Danish colonisation which seem to have radiated from the Wash, but with the indications of early Norwegian adventure and power. One such indication, of really intense interest, is the old Chester Church of St. Olave, in Bridge Street. This warrior-saint, whose career was so marked in the thousandth year after Christ, has left his name to be grouped on this spot in historical remembrance, with the earlier names of Werburgh and Oswald. But as we examine the coast of Wirrall other evidence comes into view which cannot be mistaken. These are the names of places, such as the Ness, and Neston, and Thurstaston : and especially those which have a termination commonly reckoned to be an infallible Norwegian mark, such as Irby, Frankby, Pensby,

M

Greasby, and Kirby. Of the last of these names, too, Dr. Hume
has truly observed, in his work on the western extremity of Wirrall,
that it is an indication of a fixed Christian settlement of the North-
men. To these must be added the "hoes," as the sandhills on
the extremity of this coast are called, reminding us of the "hows"
that we find in the Lake Country, among the "fells" and "forces"
which are true reminiscences of Norway. It appears, moreover—
to turn to testimony of another kind—that recent scientific observation is bringing to view "kichen-middens" in the immediate neighbourhood of the Ness and Neston. But we must now pass to the
opposite side of the estuary, and to subjects of a different kind.

In an earlier chapter, Holywell and Basingwerk, which are nearly
opposite to Neston, were named as concentrating in themselves a
large amount of the interest of the Flintshire shore; and, first, some
attention should be given to the lead-mines of this district and its
trade in lead. A considerable part of this bank of the Dee has,
so to speak, a singularly metallic and chemical aspect. This is caused
by the smelting works at Bagillt, and by the manufactories of vitriol
and other evil products of civilisation, near Flint. But—to limit
ourselves to the question of lead—the thought of this metal, in this
district, carries us over a wide range of history, and brings us in
contact with a very active modern commerce. It is clear, from the
large amount of *scoria* which has been discovered, and from other
evidence, that the Romans worked this part of the coast diligently;
and in thinking of their mining operations, the mind wonders how
such results could be accomplished without gunpowder. The reign
of Queen Elizabeth was a marked epoch in reference to this industry
in Flintshire; and ever since that time the finding and exporting and
smelting of lead have been prominent facts on this shore. One of
the local peculiarities of the case, which seems to be unique, is the
mode in which the lead-market is conducted at Holywell. Notices
of the quantity and quality of the metal on sale are forwarded to
managers of lead-works; samples are sent and tested; the purchasers

meet at Holywell on a fixed Thursday in every month; the samples
are ticketed; the prices offered are written on pieces of paper, which
are placed in a glass: the highest bidders are, of course, successful;
and the ceremony ends with a friendly lunch.

These "ticketings," however, as they are called, at Holywell, are

The Sands of Dee from above Bagillt.

not by any means the chief reason why the place is memorable.
There was a time when it was one of the most famous spots in
North-Western Europe. Many sacred wells had a high reputation
in Wales, but Holywell outshone them all. Pilgrimages from all

parts flocked to this unfailing fountain of pure water. Among these pilgrims was King James II. Pope Martin V. had connected indulgences with visits of this kind. The architecture above and around the well still recalls the munificence and devotion of the mother of

Well and Chapel of Holywell.

King Henry VII. As an illustration of the widespread belief in the efficacy of St. Winifred's Well, the following story may be quoted :—"A poor widow at Kidderminster, in Worcestershire, had long been lame and bedridden, when she sent a single penny to

Holywell, to be given to the first poor body the person should meet with there ; and at the very time it was given at Holywell the patient arose in perfect health at Kidderminster." It is very strange that the intensity of faith in this case, as in some other similar instances, ancient and modern, seems to have been precisely in proportion to the absence of evidence. No one can assign any date for the alleged facts of St. Winifred's life, death, and recovery. She is not, like St Oswald or St. Werburgh, who have been mentioned before, a person historically known to have been distinctly connected with the circumstances of a definite time, however that history may have been incrusted with legend ; nor can any writer, contemporary or nearly contemporary, be quoted in attestation of one of the most marvellous stories ever related.

The close neighbourhood of this well probably led, at a very early date, to the founding of some kind of religious house at Basingwerk. The ruins, however,

Chancel of Holywell Chapel.

which are found there are those of a Cistercian abbey of the same date as the older parts of Valle Crucis. Basingwerk deserves more space than has yet been given to it in these descriptive chapters. Its remains, indeed, and its situation are far inferior to those of the other chief ruined abbey of the Dee, which has just been named : still it is more palpably associated than the other with the river : and the views over the sands through broken fragments of its

masonry, intermingled with dark sycamores, tend to give us a sense
of the wide influence once exerted by this religious house; for we
find that lands on the opposite shore, at West Kirby, belonged to
Basingwerk.   To that point we must now turn.   If we needed poetry

Ruins of Basingwerk Abbey.

or legend to carry our thoughts across this broad tract from the
Welsh to the Cheshire shore, we should find no lack of either.
Canon Kingsley's ballad concerning "the Sands of Dee" is universally known; and in Bradshaw's life of St. Werburgh is a story
of the marvellous rescue, by that saint's intercession, of the son of

Hugh Lupus from the Welsh, through the sudden raising up of the "Constable's Sands." This story, too, is the more to our purpose just now, because the patronage of West Kirby church became the cause of a conflict between the monks of Basingwork and the

West Kirby and Hilbree Island.

monks of St. Werburgh, the cause being decided in favour of the latter.

The view obtained from the high ground above West Kirby includes much that might easily entice us into long dissertations. And, first, there is directly before us, and very near, Hilbree Island, with its smaller attendant island, and its Eye-Mark and Beach-Mark. As an element in every view of the opening of the Estuary of the Dee, this feature is remarkable and distinctive. Physically, too, and in its relation to the mainland, it deserves very careful attention. The water in the channel between is, even in high tides, shallow, and at low tide it entirely disappears. We can say of Hilbree Island, as an old writer said of Lindisfarne, "It is an island but twice a day, embraced by Neptune only at the full Tydes, and twice a day shakes hands with Great Brittayne." Like Lindisfarne, too, in another respect—as also like Iona, and like Lerins, on the south coast of France—Hilbree is one of the sacred islands of early times. It was an anchorite on this rocky solitary spot who gave the advice which led to that wonder of the "Constable's Sands" which has just been mentioned. A stone cross from this place is preserved in a Liverpool museum. The cell of St. Hildeburgha became connected with St. Werburgh's Abbey in Chester; and, through a curious freak of ecclesiastical history, this little spot of sheep-pasture, with its two houses, is still part of St. Oswald's parish in that city. The beneficent use to which the island is now devoted must not be forgotten. The *school* of buoys (and literally the pun here inevitably suggested was once made the means of turning a laugh upon H.M. Inspector on a visit to Hoylake) is here kept, for securing the perpetual marking out of the navigable channels at the mouth of the Dee. Here, too, is the Lifeboat, which saved large numbers from drowning before it was brought to this place, and which has since done much similar noble service, through the exertions of the gallant crew, summoned by a signal in the night from the mainland.

The members of the Lifeboat crew live at Hoylake; and for this reason alone it would be essential to mention this sea-coast village, before closing this short history of the Dee. But for other reasons also the extremity of Wirrall is well worthy of the most careful attention. In the sand and soil near the edge of the sea, on this part of the coast, are manifest and copious proofs of most curious changes, both physical and historical. The remains of a submerged forest show that the trees on this peninsula were even more abundant than they are now ; and relics of human civilisation, in great variety, are proofs of the presence here of a considerable population, through long periods of time. Some parts, too, of the present population must be reckoned among the curiosities of the neighbourhood. To hear of a vigorous and energetic woman in this place (the words were once literally used), that she was "the biggest scrat in all Hoylake," would cause perplexity to a stranger; but the phrase would soon be understood by those who have seen such women, with their rakes at the ends of long poles, scratching up the shellfish on the shore.

If the cocklers of Hoylake are well worthy of our attention, so too are its open-sea fishermen. It is probable that some of their sailing-boats will be conspicuously in view, as we look, from the place where we stand, over the wide expanse of water, towards the point of Air, beyond which we see, to the right, the great Orme's Head, and other receding headlands of Wales, with some of the heights of the Snowdonian range rising behind and above. This prospect brings into the mind a touching poem, of wonderful beauty, by one of the greatest of poets; for here it was, on some part of the Welsh sea-coast beyond the mouth of the Dee, that the shipwreck took place which led to Milton's "Lycidas." In the earliest of these chapters, some remarks were made on Milton's love of rivers. In "Lycidas" this feeling is very observable. Besides Arethusa and the Alpheius we find here (and what epithets could be more true to the facts?) "the swift Hebrus," and the "smooth-sliding Mincius, crowned with vocal reeds,"—and finally, the river of the poet's own college days, and the college days of his friend Edward King, whose irreparable loss he is here deploring, "slow-footing Camus,"

"His mantle hoary and his bonnet sedge."

It is not superfluous to say, once more, that this is the poem containing that phrase, "wizard stream," in reference to the Dee, which, since Milton's days, has been classical.

Thus we end, for the present, our survey of the "aspect" and "history" of the Dee. Of its various topics of interest, those which have been touched at all in these pages have been dealt with far too slightly, and many have been omitted altogether. Among subjects which under a fuller treatment would invite attention—to limit ourselves to those that have reference to the Estuary alone— are such as these : the history of Hawarden in connection with the Civil Wars and the varied events which bridge over the time between Charles I. and James II. ; the circumstances under which a vast amount of land on the opposite side of the stream has been redeemed from the sea ; the canal which, by an artificial water-way, besides that which is natural, connects Chester with Llangollen ; the habits of the salmon of the Dee, and the regulations of the salmon-fishery ; the peculiarities of that population of Neston and Parkgate which lives by collecting cockles and mussels, and which is not less worthy of study than the corresponding population of Hoylake. This mere enumeration shows how far the subject is from having reached the point of exhaustion.

Enough, however, has been written in these twelve short essays to justify what was said at the outset concerning the attractiveness of rivers. To the *artist* a river must be alluring, by reason of its animated variety of beautiful scenes,—to the *naturalist*, by reason of its wealth of animal and vegetable life within its waters and upon its banks,—to the *historian*, because of his study an essential part is geography, and here are furnished the most instructive lessons of geography. With the *sympathetic lover of his kind*, who must be reckoned higher than any of these, though he need be neither artist nor naturalist nor historian, the interest of a river reaches a point superior still. For a river, like a great cathedral, is linked by the closest ties to both the past and the present, with this great advantage, that it is not liable to decay. Its perpetually flowing life — always new and always old — binds together, and, as long as the world lasts, will continue to bind, successive generations of men.

Fishing-boat leaving the Dee.

APPENDIX.

N account of the Dee would be very imperfect if it did not include a notice of the salmon-fisheries. These, in very recent times, have increased enormously. The returns of 1884 and 1885 are not before me ; but, in 1882, 10,935 were returned as being caught in the river, averaging 10 lbs. each ; and the following year the returns showed an increase of 565 fish, averaging a similar weight. The abundance or otherwise of a season would seem to lie in a province that so far is out of our knowledge. We know for certainty, indeed, that pollution of water is bound to bring scarcity, and, if persevered in, is certain to extinguish this noble fish. But, even where all known conditions are favourable, or where they are otherwise, the success of the fisheries is uncertain.

Thus, the season of 1884 was an exceptionally poor one for the Dee, and 1885 only a very little better ; while the present year, 1886, is so far no better than 1884. Still, even here there is no room for discouragement, as the improvement in the fisheries has been steady (though with some few drawbacks, such as we meet with in all harvests) since the Government took up the question of the general fishing laws.

The Blue Book of 1883 puts the case very concisely. The Inspector, in his very interesting report, says : " As in the case of individual rivers, so in the case of the fisheries generally, the unexpected occurrence of a season of almost unexampled abundance, like that of 1883, is as little to be accounted for as a season of scarcity. The circumstances under which salmon-fishing was conducted in 1883 were almost the same as those that prevailed in any year since the present Act came into force. In years of scarcity it has been customary to allege 'over-fishing' as the cause, and there is just as much reason for attributing abundance to previous 'under-fishing.' But there is no evidence that there has been in recent years any abatement of nets in any of the districts in which there was an abundance of salmon last year; and it would, therefore, be only reasonable to have expected a continuance of bad seasons, instead of an improvement in the yield of salmon." But the Inspector adds that there was no diminution in the yield during the years of plenty, for the exceeding plenty of 1883 followed upon a great increase in 1882.

The Inspector says that latterly he has had his attention directed to several items that are worth much further consideration. One thing that he mentions is very clear. In order to understand the supply question more fully we should know the meteorological conditions after spawning. One thing is certain, that the best spawning seasons may be followed by a dearth of salmon, at the time when grisle and two-year-old salmon might be looked for, as all conservators of the Dee will tell us; and the Inspector advocates the adoption of more complete meteorological reports. It may possibly be worth while to notice here that the atmospheric conditions which favour the growth and maturity of salmon pink also carry dangers with them.

Every schoolboy knows that fish bite better some days than others, and, indeed, the sky and barometer are closely, if not always intelligently, studied before an excursion. That "When thunder is about fish will not take," is as generally believed as that, "When the wind is from the south, it blows the hook into the fish's mouth;" and, subject to other laws, there is much truth in both these sayings. If the salmon fry prosper and gain in health and activity, the coarser fish of the Dee, such as chub, perch, and pike, do the same, and are, as anglers say, "on the feed." Good fishing weather, therefore, such as delights the angler, is death for the samlets which swarm over the rippling shallows of the Dee, the Severn, and the Wye. The coarser fish hunt them to death in shoals, and prove even more ubiquitous than anglers or nets. It seems almost impossible to understand how, in some cases, any salmon at all escape. The writer remembers a case of this kind occurring in the wilds of Canada : the salmon had to run the gauntlet of the outlet of a lake through which a river passed. This outlet consisted of a bay of several acres in extent, and was literally paved with the dusky backs of pike waiting for the salmon to ascend from the sea, some thirty-five or forty miles distant. In Canada, these fish are rightly called vermin, and are, where possible, hunted down. However, salmon did, in great numbers, manage to pass the Rubicon, though it must have fared ill with their progeny when they descended to the sea.

The visitor to Chester will be exceedingly astonished to see the fishermen in the middle of the ancient city plying their nets and bringing out noble silvery salmon only a few hundred yards from the stalls where they will soon be exposed for sale. Indeed, I once saw a fish of not more than twelve pounds weight on a slab in Northgate Street, which suddenly showed signs of life, and sprang off the counter; and so strong was it in its last battle for life as to throw itself out of the fishmonger's arms.

The system employed at Chester, and in its district, for catching them is this: There are two men that jointly own a boat and all the netting and contrivances that pertain to salmon-fishing; one of them holds the ends of the net, while the other crosses the stream; they then bring the net round in a sweep. The net is some sixty yards in length, and its lower end is weighted, while the other is supported by cork floats. When the boat has made its sweep round, the men begin to pull in the ends of the net, thus gradually decreasing the circle and hemming the fish into a smaller compass, until the whole of it is gathered in and the salmon extracted from the last coil. This operation may be seen any day within a stone's throw of Chester Old Bridge.

The numbers of salmon given above must not be supposed to include the great quantity captured by rod and line in the upper waters, of which it is obvious that no account can be kept. The principal stations for rod-fishing are Llangollen—though in this case some distance must be travelled before the fishing-grounds are reached—Llansaintfraidd, Llandullo, and Llanderfel; and the affluents of the river are almost as well stocked with salmon as the stream itself.

Much of the salmon, however, that is sold in Chester as Dee salmon comes in reality from Ireland, and some even from Norway. The Dee salmon is often called the best in England, but that perhaps is its character locally. There can be no doubt, of course, that the clear waters and the abundant food give this fish an excellent chance; but another reason is that salmon are always best close to the stream where they are caught, just as apples are always best in the orchards where they are grown; the fact being that both suffer by the shaking attendant upon a long railway journey.

Sometimes, as in the Ribble, the quality of the fish has deteriorated, and the reason is, that while formerly there was an abundance of clear fresh water, latterly the water has been to some extent polluted by reason of the proximity to it; of manufacturing works; the fish are, therefore, less active and strong than formerly; and when the pollutions increase (which must be the case in the absence of any statutory prohibition) salmon will soon disappear entirely from the river.

One of the most interesting sights in the whole course of the river Dee is the salmon ascending the weir at Chester, which is a very ancient dam to store up the waters of the Dee, which it does for miles, and thus secures a constant water-power for the Chester mills. When, in very dry weather, only a few inches of water flow over any portion of the river, the fresh-run fish from the sea make violent efforts to pass it; and nothing can give such an idea of the power and vigour of a salmon as to see it, with violent contortions, force its way against the stream for some yards up the steep bar, and, even then, only about half covered with water. Sometimes the fish are driven back, but they speedily recover themselves in the pool below, and make another effort, in the end being successful. A series of tanks or steps has been adopted at some of the Dee obstructions, but they have not been a success. The salmon suspect them, even though placed for their special advantage. The time-honoured quotation of "timeo Danaos" would seem even to have reached the *salmonidæ*.

There can be no doubt, however, that, with the new protective laws, in conjunction with the science which is brought to bear on the subject, the salmon supply is well on its way to increase both in quantity and certainty.

PRINTED BY J. S. VIRTUE AND CO., LIMITED, CITY ROAD, LONDON.

ILLUSTRATED GIFT BOOKS.

Small 4to, cloth gilt, gilt edges, 15s. each.

Switzerland: its Mountains, Valleys, Lakes, and

Rivers. With nearly 200 Illustrations.

" An exceedingly appropriate gift-book for those who like picturesque description with equally charming illustrations."—*Yorkshire Post.*

Rome, the Eternal City: its Churches, Monuments,

Art, and Antiquities. With nearly 300 Illustrations.

" It is much to be recommended. It gives almost a perfect idea of the Eternal City on the seven hills as it has been revolutionized by municipal Haussmannizing and swept by new brooms.—*The Times.*

The Rhine: from its Source to the Sea. With

nearly 200 Illustrations.

" A capital book to revive memories of summer trips."—*Saturday Review.*

Italy: its Rivers, its Lakes, its Cities, its Arts.

With nearly 200 Illustrations.

" Amply illustrated with 164 woodcuts, many of them of full-page size and well engraved . . . not only forms a most useful companion for travellers to the Sunny South, but well deserves a prominent place in a lady's library, on her drawing-room table, and amongst her Christmas presents."—*The Queen.*

Cloth gilt, gilt edges, £1 1s.

The Riviera, both Eastern and Western. With 24

Page Illustrations, and nearly 150 in the Text, including Descriptions and Illustrations of the following towns, among many others :—Nice, Cannes, Mentone, San Remo, &c.

" The book is one of a superior character, and the illustrations are numerous and tasteful ; an excellent map of the Riviera is prefixed to it, which is a constant help to the reader."
—*Illustrated London News.*

Small imperial 4to, cloth gilt, gilt edges, £1 1s.

Jerusalem, the Holy City. By Colonel Sir CHARLES

WILSON. With about 80 Engravings on Steel and Wood.

" No work we know gives so good an idea of the Holy City with its sacred surroundings and its historical remains."—*Times.*

" From every point of view it is a book which deserves high commendation."—*Guardian.*

" Enriched with a great many capital woodcuts of ancient buildings and historic sites of all kinds."—*Athenæum.*

" The whole book is possibly the best monograph extant on the antiquities, architecture, and traditions of the sacred capital."—*Daily Telegraph.*

LONDON :   J. S. VIRTUE & CO., LIMITED, 26, IVY LANE, E.C.

www.ingramcontent.com/pod-product-compliance
Lightning Source LLC
Chambersburg PA
CBHW030836270326
41928CB00007B/1082